EDUCATOR'S DESKBOOK
OF
IDEAS AND ACTIVITIES
FROM AWARD-WINNING TEACHERS

EDUCATOR'S DESKBOOK
OF
IDEAS AND ACTIVITIES
FROM AWARD-WINNING TEACHERS

RUTH ANNE TSCHUDIN

PARKER PUBLISHING COMPANY, INC., WEST NYACK, NEW YORK

© 1980, *by*

Ruth Anne Tschudin

Library of Congress Cataloging in Publication Data

Tschudin, Ruth Anne,
    Educator's deskbook of ideas and activities from
award-winning teachers.

    Includes bibliographical references and index.
    1. Lesson planning--Handbooks, manuals, etc.
2. Creative thinking (Education)--Handbooks, manuals,
etc. 3. Activity programs in education--Handbooks,
manuals, etc. I. Title.
LB1027.T79   371.3   80-103
ISBN 0-13-240747-7

Printed in the United States of America

HOW THIS BOOK CAN
HELP YOU BECOME
A MORE EFFECTIVE TEACHER

If you would like to know what many of our finest teachers are doing—what they have in common, what distinguishes them from others, and what good ideas they have to offer—then this book is for you!

It gathers together great ideas from great teachers—on the basis of *proven* differences between "average" teachers and teachers you would rate "A+." The activities and teaching techniques described in this book have been tested, validated, and recommended by outstanding contemporary educators. These teachers have been recognized as superior by principals and colleagues, spotlighted in newspapers and educational periodicals, or nominated for state and national "Teacher of the Year" awards.[1]*

The author's extensive survey of more than 300 exceptional teachers and a control group of "other teachers" has yielded statistical evidence that there are indeed attitudes and practices which "make the difference." This book explains the ones that count and illustrates them with a galaxy of specific examples.

You will not be burdened with theories that *should* work. You will be offered realities that *do* work, as America's highly acclaimed teachers reveal, through this book, many of those small but vital secrets which have helped to spell S-U-C-C-E-S-S for them.

Some cases in point:

- One teacher found it increasingly difficult to cope with a rash of student misbehavior, and realized her reactions to the situa-

---

*See Section "NOTES" at end of book.

tions—and particularly her interactions with the worst offenders—
were "mushrooming" rather than diminishing her problems.
She hit upon an approach (see Chapter 11) that immediately
improved her rapport with the class, nipped most discipline
problems in the bud, and helped to bring out the best in both
herself *and* the students.

- Another teacher was, at one point, ready to abandon homework
  completely—on the grounds that it was not making positive
  educational contributions and was, in fact, fostering negative
  attitudes. Was she expecting too much from her elementary
  students? She made one last attempt to interest them in doing
  homework, using a type of "free-rein" assignment (Chapter 12).
  Not only did her students exhibit a refreshing eagerness at the
  prospect of such an assignment, but the quality, volume, and
  diversity of the homework they submitted were unprecedented.

- A Midwestern teacher noticed that "testing jitters" were having
  adverse effects upon his students, both emotionally and academically. He remedied the situation by putting humorous
  "relief valves" right into his tests (Chapter 13). The results?
  His tests more adequately reflected the students' abilities because
  much of that paralyzing nervousness was alleviated, and students
  actually began to look forward to tests to see what little "fun
  items" would be included among the serious ones.

- What does a teacher do when assigned an unusually run-down,
  depressing classroom? Believing strongly that her students should
  be greeted with a warm, cheerful room as well as a caring, conscientious teacher, this particular person went right to work.
  Before school opened, she prepared a variety of eye-appealing
  displays for the classroom—in addition to planning an exciting
  curriculum (Chapter 4). So uplifting was the educational environment she created that even suspended students were known
  to sneak up a back stairway so they would not have to miss
  her class.

This is the type of real-life, productive material you will find
in this book. Browse through it. Turn to any of its fifteen chapters.
You will readily spot practical guidelines, down-to-earth teaching
ideas, and helpful information you can put to *direct and immediate
use* no matter what, where, or whom you teach. There are literally
hundreds of classroom-tested ideas which can help you to:

- stress goals that can turn your students' attitudes around
  by 180 degrees;

- prepare efficient teaching plans that can save you hours of needless drudgery while increasing your effectiveness;
- tap the virtually limitless resources that can enhance your professional growth and add new richness to your curriculum;
- motivate even your most apathetic students to become interested and involved through the use of "sure fire" materials, activities, and teaching methods;
- open up a fascinating "new world" of enjoyable and enticing homework assignments;
- make testing less of a threat and more of a positive learning experience;
- streamline your record-keeping so that it is no longer such a dreaded chore;
- prevent or solve those vexing discipline problems that so often hamper the learning process; and
- develop more of those personal and professional qualities found to set top teachers apart from others.

Here is a sourcebook you will treasure—not just because it will get you thinking about the many exciting things you *can* do (and how you might do them), but because it is written with a warmth and realism that only a teacher like yourself could capture! This is not a pie-in-the-sky answer to the shortcomings of our education system, but a fun-to-read collection of *tried and true teaching tips from A+ educators* who would like to see every teacher "make the grade."

Read it, enjoy it, and refer to it often for the kind of information *and* inspiration that will help you to become a more effective teacher.

DEDICATION

To *you*, the teacher . . . . molder of today's youth.

ACKNOWLEDGMENTS

Now that I can finally sit back and survey the finished product, my first and foremost desire is to praise the Lord for putting this book idea in my mind and for guiding me each step of the way. Next, I would like to express my heartfelt gratitude to those special people who joined their enthusiasm with mine to make this dream a reality, namely:

Dominic Grassano, my principal, whose support in this project has made a great difference;

Carl Padovano, superintendent of the Hackensack, N.J., School System, and the members of the Hackensack Board of Education, who exhibited faith in both me and my undertaking by granting me a leave to pursue my goal;

Mary Barnett, Anne Chatfield, Hazel Goldstein, Charles T. Jones, Frank Madden, Theresa Pasadino, Mary Payson, Hilda L. Pearlman, Bobbi Rothstein, Ellen Silver, Judith Sorrenti, Carol Tenebruso, Barbara Toole, and *Mildred M. Von der Linden,* teachers who pilot-tested my questionnaire and suggested productive changes;

Harold Bloom, Thomas A. Daly, Jr., James Hessian, Bernard P. Kaminsky, Alfred Kane, Emil Massa, Richard Menhinick, Thomas N. Olsen, Mary Pramuk, Edna Roach, Frank Scatina, Constantino Scerbo, Stephen F.D. Shea, Ann Stasiewski, George Velotto, and other administrators too numerous to mention by name, who most willingly assisted;

Leanna Landsmann, Ken Bierly, and others who worked hard to condense this large work into an article, "The Secrets of A+ Teaching," for *Instructor* magazine;

Alex Dobrowolski, the A+ Teacher who "faced the nation" as a guest on the "Today Show," personifying the outstanding contemporary teacher;

Ellen Von den Deale, a dear friend, who helped and inspired me as I wrote this book;

Howard and Grace Olnowich, my parents, whose constant love and understanding have been a great source of joy;

Elisa Grace Tschudin, my darling daughter, who has been patiently sharing me with this project her entire life;

Hugo Tschudin, my beloved husband, whose steadfast encouragement and expert editorial assistance made this book possible;

And last, but far from least,

Those who made it all happen—the hundreds of teachers who took time from their already crowded schedules to respond to the extensive survey which is the basis of this book, who in many cases went far beyond what was expected by providing samples, answering lengthy lists of additional questions, and taking part in detailed interviews. These are truly the "stars" of the book:

* * * PARTICIPATING TEACHERS * * *

KEY

n	=	nominee for state Teacher of the Year
T	=	State Teacher of the Year
NT	=	National Teacher of the Year
k	=	kindergarten teacher
el	=	elementary teacher (grades 1–6)
jhs	=	junior high school teacher (grades 7–9)
hs	=	high school teacher (grades 10–12)

Juanita Alexander (n, Oklahoma)
Ruth Allar (New Jersey, jhs)
Connie Anderson (n, Colorado, el)
Therese Anglin (New York, el)
Mary Ann Anthony (Connecticut, k)
Adah M. Arthur (T, Arkansas, hs)
Edgar Askew (New Jersey, jhs)
Martha Ayers (n, Illinois, hs)

Wally Bain (n, Florida, hs)
Ida Lou Balentine (Alabama, el)
Richard H. Barber (n, Arizona, jhs)
Gale L. Barnes (n, Nebraska, hs)
Ellen Barraco (New York, el)
Ladd L. Bausch (n, Arizona, hs)
W.H. Beckmeyer (n, illinois, hs)
Victor Bell (n, Illinois, hs)

ACKNOWLEDGMENTS

Carl R. Berg (Illinois, el)
June Betsworth (California, el)
Marjorie Bicking (Delaware, el)
Inza Biggerstaff (Kentucky, el)
R. Biros (New Jersey, hs)
Dorothy P. Blanchard (Connecticut, el)
Wallace D. Boblit (n, Oklahoma, hs)
Harry Boggs (n, New Mexico, jhs and hs)
Edward E. Bowman (n, New Jersey, jhs)
Elizabeth Braden (n, Illinois, el)
Mary Ann Brady (n, Tennessee, jhs)
Jane Brake (n, Arizona, hs)
Caroline Bauer (New Jersey, jhs)
Josephine P. Brown (California, el)
Maureen Buckmiller (New Jersey, el)
James Burgett (n, Illinois, jhs)
Elinor T. Butler (New Hampshire, hs)

Mrs. Jett B. Campbell (n, Oklahoma, hs)
Ruth Campopiano (T, New Jersey, hs)
Ralph Caputo (n, Arizona, el)
Emily Pritchard Carey (New Jersey, el)
Barbara E. Carlson (n, Pennsylvania, el)
Patricia Ceballos (n, Arizona, el)
Minnie Belle Churchill (n, Oklahoma, hs)
Myrtle Collins (T, West Virginia, el)
Mary C. Commers (Nebraska, hs)
Pauline Connors (T, Rhode Island, el)
Santa Corrado (n, New Jersey, el)
Joy R. Cosgrove (New Jersey, el)
Harold I. Cotler (New Jersey, el)
Jerry L. Craven (n, Illinois, hs)
Roberta Cromwell (New Jersey, hs)
Michael C. Cupell (n, Arizona, hs)
R.K. Curtis (New Jersey, hs)

Anthony D'Ambrosio (n, New Jersey, hs)
Mrs. J. D'Ambrosio (New Jersey, jhs)
Ann D. Davies (Nebraska, el)
Barbara Jean Dean (T, Indiana, el)
Lily DeCleir (T, Idaho, el)
Carol M. DeLorenzo (n, New Jersey, el)
Mardene D. Derry (n, Illinois, jhs)
Donald R. DeVries (New Jersey, jhs)
Julia A. Dice (n, Oklahoma, hs)
Max Dicken (n, Colorado, el)
Alex Dobrowolski (New Jersey, jhs)
Joyce Dow (n, Vermont, el)
Susan Downey (New Jersey, el)
Mary E. Duffy (T, Texas, jhs)

Jane P. Eddins (n, Wyoming, el)
Donna L. Egy (Iowa, el)
Emily Ehm (n, Illinois, jhs)

Ruth Elwell (Nebraska, k)
Frank H. Estavillo (n, Arizona, el)

Gladys Farrenkopf (New Jersey, hs)
Jeffrey N. Felz (California, el)
Maxel J. Ferguson (Alaska, el)
Mario Fierros (n, Arizona, hs)
Lorraine A. Fill (New Jersey, el)
Lillian Flanagan (Vermont, el)
Margaret D. Fleming (New Jersey, hs)
Eleanor Foley (n, Colorado, el)
Angela G. Folli (n, New Jersey, el)
Herman L. Forbes (T, North Carolina, el)
Mike Ford (T, Oregon, jhs)
Robert R. Foschini (New Jersey, el)
Harry Foster (Washington, el)
Rose Fraden (California, el)
Dorothy Frazier (Oklahoma, hs)
Ina Frazier (n, Pennsylvania, el)

Dr. Girolama Garner (Arizona, el)
Don Gibson (n, Minnesota, jhs)
Allen Gilbert (n, Oklahoma, jhs and hs)
Kathryn A. Gillespie (n, Illinois, el)
Gladys M. Glever (Delaware, k)
Robert Glover (n, Illinois, hs)
Donna Goldsmith (New Jersey, jhs)
Robert E. Goldsmith (New Jersey, jhs)
Lita Grabeklis (n, Illinois, el)
Rebecca Guess (n, New Jersey, el)
Sally E. Gunerman (Wisconsin, hs)
Helen B. Guptill (n, Arizona, jhs)
Hubert W. Hadorn (n, South Dakota, jhs)
Carolyn C. Haines (New Jersey, el)
Jessie M. Hamilton (California, k)
Marie D. Hanlon (n. New Jersey, el)
Doris Harder (n, Nebraska, hs)
Jean S. Harney (T, Kentucky, el)
Linda Harper (Georgia, el)
Mary M. Harris (Massachusetts, el)
Elsie F. Hart (n, Illinois, k)
Winnefred M. Haugland (Vermont, el)
Ann S. Hawley (New Jersey, el)
Sally E. Hedges (n, Oklahoma, hs)
Don Helgren (n, Nebraska, hs)
Edward C. Helwick, Jr. (T, California, hs)
W. Charles Henderson (n, Oklahoma, hs)
Essie Kirkland Hendley (New Jersey, el)
Robert Herold (n, Vermont, hs)
Beth Herrington (n, Oklahoma, el)
Erma Hesterberg (n, Illinois, hs)
Charleen Hickey (T, Arizona, hs)
William F. Higdon (T, Missouri, hs)
Sheryl Hinman (Illinois, jhs)

Mary C. Holden (T, Arkansas, el)
Donovan J. Holderness (n, New Mexico, hs)
Richard J. Hoptar (n, Florida, hs)
Gunnar Horn (T, Nebraska, hs)
Sue Houston (Arizona, el)
Marian Howard (n, Colorado, el)
Dr. Charles Y. Hoyt (n, Arizona, hs)
Clara Humphrey (T, Kentucky, hs)
Clida Hunter (n, Oklahoma, hs)
Pat Hurst (n, Oklahoma, hs)
Dan Hyer (New Jersey, jhs)

Dorothy A. Jacob (Georgia, k)
Agnes P. Jacobs (n, New Jersey, el)
Louisa Johnson (New Jersey, hs)
Shirley A. Johnson (n, Arizona, jhs and hs)

Robert Keane (New Jersey, hs)
Katherine H. Kearney (n, New Jersey, el)
Anne S. Kelly (California, el)
Betty Kenny (n, New Jersey, hs)
Mildred Kerr (n, Oklahoma, hs)
Alice Kihn (New Jersey, el)
Su Chon Kin (n, Hawaii, el)
Lenora Kimborough (n, Illinois, hs)
Frances A. Kiser (T, North Carolina, hs)
Barton L. Kline (n, Nebraska, jhs and hs)
Doris Kneppel (n, New Jersey, el)
Harry H. Koch (n, Illinois, hs)
Roger Kolsrud (T, North Dakota, hs)
Ann Koprowicz (n, Illinois, k)
Eva Korth (New Jersey, el)
A. Kuchar (New Jersey, el)

Connie M. Lacher (n, Minnesota, el)
Renee LaCorbinere (New York, el)
Hugh T. Lane (New Jersey, hs)
Margaret LaVassor (n, Minnesota, hs)
Rene L. Lavergneau (New Jersey, hs)
Lola Lehman (n, Illinois, el)
Diane Lewis (New Jersey, jhs)
Sarah Lilja (n, Pennsylvania, el)
Mrs. Virgil M. Linderoth (n, Minnesota, el)
Diane Liskow (n, Minnesota, el)
Johnnie A. Littlefield (n, Tennessee, el)
Wendie S. Liu (n, Hawaii, jhs)
Estela Lopez (n, Colorado, k)
Marilyn Loppnow (n, Minnesota, el)
Lynn Lothian (New Jersey, el)
Celine Lujan (n, New Mexico, el)
Patricia Lynch (New Jersey, el)

Joan Macey (New York, el)
Robert MacNeely (n, New Mexico, hs)
Dr. Jean D'Arcy Maculaitis (n, New Jersey, jhs and hs)
Elaine F. Magee (T, Virginia, hs)
E. Dean Makie (n, Wyoming, jhs)
Gil Marshall (Maryland, jhs and hs)
Michael Mason (Illinois, el)
H.S. Mathe (n, Arizona, hs)
Diane Mazzei (New Jersey, el)
Mary A. McCabe (n, Utah, el)
Olivia N. McMillan (n, Alabama, el)
Margaret Mecca (T, Wyoming, hs)
Opal B. Melvin (T, Mississippi, hs)
Fred Miller, Jr. (n, Arizona, el and jhs)
Virginia Minker (n, Oklahoma, el)
Jerome Minkewicz (New Jersey, hs)
Edwin R. Mitchell (n, New Jersey, el)
Gail B. Mitchell (n, Illinois, hs)
Earl J. Montgomery (n, Illinois, jhs)
Barbara T. Moore (n, Alabama, el)
Shirley Moore (New Jersey, el)
Hazel C. Morton (Delaware, el)
Miriam Moskowitz (New Jersey, jhs)
Norma Munson (n, Illinois, hs)
Catherine Murphy (n, New Jersey, el)
John F. Musser (n, Colorado, el)

Audrey Nagel (New Jersey, el)
Russell Nelson (Oregon, jhs)
Ann Nicoll (n, New Jersey, hs)
Tom C. Nicholson (T, Illinois, hs)
Mrs. Jessie Norwood (n, Illinois, jhs)
Margy Nurik (New Jersey, jhs)

Lee G. Oberparleiter (n, New Jersey, hs)
Josephine J. Owen (Maryland, jhs)
Moke C. Owens (n, Illinois, jhs)

Billy J. Pack (n, Tennessee, jhs)
Joseph D. Paradise (n, New Jersey, el)
Gloryl Parchert (n, Illinois, el)
Barbara Payne (n, Tennessee, jhs)
Margaret J. Payne (n, Illinois, el)
Brenda Pena (New York, el)
Norene Perisi (Michigan, k)
Sylvia Pierce (Alabama, el)
James C. Pollman (n, South Dakota, hs)
Jean Pryor (New Jersey, jhs)
Alice Purdes (n, Illinois, el)

Donna Quan (California, el)
Mary Ann Quinn (California, el)

Mrs. Wayne Reisch (Indiana, el)

Catherine Reuter (n, Colorado, el)
Claire Y. Reyes (n, Hawaii, hs)
Gary C. Rhiel (Ohio, jhs)
Alva Rinehart (n, Oklahoma, el)
Keith L. Rogers (T, Colorado, el)
Ernest Rondeau (n, New Mexico, hs)
Irene Rosen (New York, el)
Bob Roszko (New Jersey, hs)
Bobbie Rothstein (New Jersey, el)
Margaret J. Rourke (n, Arizona, hs)
Virginia K. Rowe (T, Virginia, el)
Jan Rusowicz (New Jersey, el)
Janet L. Ryan (Massachusetts, el)

Chris Sabo (New Jersey, el)
Lugarda Sandoval (n, New Mexico, el)
Kent Schipper (n, Arizona, jhs)
Larry Schloer (n, Minnesota, jhs)
Esther Schmidt (n, Minnesota, el)
Fred Schott (New Jersey, jhs)
Sarah Schreiner (n, Oklahoma, k)
Frank Scheunemann (n, New Jersey, jhs)
John M. Selig (n, Alabama, hs)
Frances M. Sherlock (Massachusetts, k)
Faye Shaw (T, Florida, el)
Lettie Siddens (Missouri, el)
Margaret Simpson (West Virginia, el)
Patricia Sink (West Virginia, el)
Lois K. Smith (Ohio, el)
Dr. Cy Sommer (n, New Jersey, hs)
Joe E. Spence (n, Tennessee, hs)
Audrey Stanton (n, Minnesota, el)
Kay Stapleton (Texas, hs)
James Sterr (n, Arizona)
Jane A. Stevens (n, Oklahoma, el)
Diane A. Sypher (California, el)

Mrs. Thomas Thirsk (New Hampshire, el)
Carol Thollander (California, el)
Charles Thompson (n, Colorado, hs)

Helen Tieger (California, jhs)
James P. Tierney (n, New Jersey, jhs)
F.W. Tietsworth (New Jersey, hs)
Nancy Thompkins (Ohio, el)
Ida Mary Torzella (n, New Jersey, k)
Ruth Townsend (Iowa, el)
Lyllian M. Tubbs (T, Mississippi, el)
Doris Turner (n, Illinois, el)
Ruth Turner (n, Illinois, el)

Vincent J. Vespe (n, New Jersey, hs)
Rolando P. Vigneault (New Hampshire, hs)
Mary Vucichevich (n, Arizona, el)

Robert R. Walton (n, Minnesota, hs)
Wanda Ward (New York, el)
Sharon A. Watson (n, Minnesota, k)
Barbara Webster (n, New Jersey, jhs)
Charles W. Webster (n, Colorado, jhs)
Maralene Wesner (T, Oklahoma, el)
Downer White (n, Arizona, jhs)
Wanda White (n, Oklahoma, el)
Cecilia Whitehouse (n, New Jersey, hs)
Willard C. Widerberg (NT, Illinois, jhs)
Edith Widicus (n, Illinois, el)
Betty B. Willey (n, New Jersey, el)
Donald R. Wilson (n, Arizona, hs)
Roberta Wilson (New Jersey, el)
Mrs. Ray Winkler (n, Illinois, el)
Bob Winter (n, South Dakota, hs)
Florence Wise (n, Oklahoma, el)
Rinna Wolfe (California, el)
Louise M. Woodall (Alabama, jhs)
Mary D. Wren (New Jersey, jhs)

Tom Zaccone (New Jersey, hs)
Emilie Zacher (n, South Dakota, el)
Robert Zakaluk (n, New Jersey, hs)
Charles Zeichner (n, New Jersey, jhs)
Verna Ziegenhagen (n, Minnesota, el)
Ann Zuzov (n, New Jersy, el)

And a hearty thank you also to those survey participants who wished to remain anonymous!

R.T.

TABLE OF CONTENTS

EDUCATOR'S DESKBOOK
OF
IDEAS AND ACTIVITIES
FROM AWARD-WINNING TEACHERS

1 HOW TO SET GOALS THAT WILL HELP YOUR STUDENTS WANT TO LEARN

What kind of difference will *you* make in your students' lives? will they remember you for the sound knowledge and practical skills you imparted to them? Will they attribute their interest in a certain subject, their love of learning, or their self-confidence to you?

When our everyday actions as teachers line up with our aspirations, we may not even have to wait around to be appreciated in retrospect. Here, for example, is a stunned but pleased parent talking on the telephone—telling a friend about a teacher who is exerting a positive, long-lasting influence on her son.

> You know, Agnes, it's really unbelievable! Last year John was indifferent about German, but this year it's a whole new ballgame!
>
> Well, it's hard to explain, but he just loves German and he can't do enough for his teacher . . .
>
> You're right, Agnes, the teacher really *is* terrific. She has high standards like last year's, but there's more warmth . . . yes, a caring. She really likes the students and tries to boost their egos *as well as* their grades.
>
> And listen to this. John was asked to bring his guitar to school to accompany their "German Song and Dance Fest." Then he ended up helping the class write an original song in German. They made up the words and he created the melody.
>
> Agnes, I've never seen anything like it! The kids are interviewing German-Americans, reading German newspapers, cooking wiener-schnitzel, and visiting patients in that German nursing home. They even spoke with a West German diplomat about world problems . . .
>
> How does he do in reading, writing, and speaking? Well, to give you an example, he translated Tante Berta's letter for us yesterday—and then answered it! He is certainly doing better than we ever thought

1

he could; and he seems to have an unquenchable thirst to do and
learn more . . .

That's right. And do you know what I like most? Not only is he
doing well in German, but he's also becoming a more confident,
thoughtful person. All I can say is *Wunderbar!* and give that teacher
an A+!

This is what this book is all about: those "A+" Teachers who, at
every grade level, make their subjects *and* their students come joyfully
alive. More than 300 of these great teachers volunteered to participate
in an extensive survey, revealing their "secrets" and describing their
teaching practices in detail. Because a large sampling of Other Teachers
also participated, we are able to compare the two groups to find
out what outstanding teachers are doing that sets them apart from
others in the teaching profession.

These survey outcomes will be presented to you, chapter by
chapter, with an abundance of practical teaching ideas which can
help you to become the teacher you would like to be.

In this chapter, top-rated teachers will show how you can turn your
students into eager learners by:

- relating studies to the "real world,"
- building students' academic confidence,
- raising student self-esteem, and
- giving students more responsibility.

ADD" LIFE" TO STUDIES WITH REAL-WORLD TIE-INS

Should schoolwork relate to the outside world? A+ Teachers
answer with an emphatic "yes" and practice what they preach by
stressing student involvement in current issues significantly more
than Other Teachers. They do this not only to prepare their students
for a responsible, productive life sometime in the future, but also to
add interest and meaning to their present classwork. Here is their
three-part strategy:

Bring news into the classroom

Mary Ann Brady uses many *newspaper-related activities* with
her ninth-grade Civics and Economics classes. The same daily paper
is used for relating either Civics or Economics to what is happening

in the world—and sometimes even the same article is studied from the two different perspectives.

Mrs. Ray Winkler uses current issues with student appeal as over-all themes for class studies involving all school subjects. A special *current events bulletin board* is a permanent feature in her classroom. Her fourth-graders help by keeping it up to date with local, state, U.S., and world news items—and daily entries for entertainment, sports, and weather. The display is often the focal point of class discussions and related small-group projects.

Margaret J. Payne makes it fun to be informed on current issues by instituting a weekly *"Current Events Quiz Day."* Each student prepares ten clues about a timely topic or a person in the news, and presents one clue at a time to the class, using the overhead projector. If the subject is guessed on the first clue, ten points are awarded to the class. The point value descends with each clue written on the transparency (9 . . . 8 . . . 7 etc.) until all are given.

Connie Anderson gets an enthusiastic response from her fourth-graders when she gives one of her *"DTT" assignments.* These are "dinner table topics" which include controversial subjects like fluoridation, pollution, cigarettes, hunting, war, flying saucers, etc. The students discuss these at home with their families and return the following day with a rich variety of facts and opinions to share with the class.

Get students to communicate, in writing, with the outside world

Ann Zuzov's second-graders often write to important people, and everyday people, in the news. They sent *sympathy cards* to Mamie Eisenhower, Mrs. Lyndon B. Johnson, and the Kennedy family when these former presidents died—and in response to their thoughtfulness received cards of thanks.

Her students also have *penpals* in their own state, other areas of the United States, and as far away as Africa. And they occasionally exchange letters with shut-ins, an adopted "grandfather," or editors of the local papers. It is not unusual for her students to write to Chambers of Commerce for information or to textbook companies to question items in the books. Ms. Zuzov admits that her greatest expense is for stamps but considers that she and her students get "full value."

During summer reading school, my third- and fourth-graders wrote many *letters requesting free materials.* Using a paperback book which listed free items currently available, the students and I designed advertising posters, like the ones in Exhibit 1-1, trying to entice each other to write for the "freebies." The letter/number code on the ads helped students to locate the proper address in our file so they could plan, type, and mail their own letters. Naturally, enthusiasm ran high each time a letter or package arrived in the mail![1]*

EXHIBIT 1-1: "WRITE-AWAY" AD POSTERS

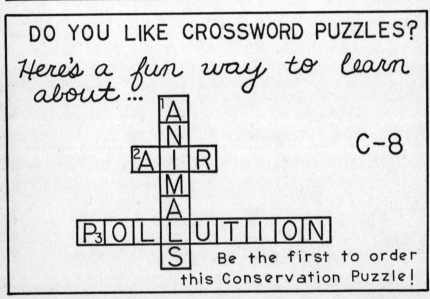

---

* See Section "NOTES" at end of book.

In an alternative high school, where Lee Oberparleiter teaches English, students prepare a *"Consumer Newsletter"* for their community. They research topics of local interest, and, through their newsletter, make the public aware of food prices at various stores, current merchandise availability, and consumer-related problems.

Make students an active part of contemporary life

Students in Edward Helwick's U.S. Government classes did more than just study about the set-up and functions of their local government. They went out and interviewed the city administrators, then compiled their original research into an a 58-page *municipal handbook.* Information on the schools, government, community history, and demography were included. It was so well done that it has been published by the city and is now used as an official informational booklet!

Kay Stapleton's high school Art students not only read and hear about contemporary artists, but they also take frequent *field trips* to art shows and museums to observe painters and craftspeople at work.

Louisa Johnson's Home Economics students put their learning "to the outside test" by preparing and serving true Colonial Thanksgiving dinners to kindergarteners and by using mass-production techniques to bake *cookies for the child welfare home* and the local day care centers.

Mary Ann Brady's junior high school students *cleaned out a local play area,* which included a creek filled with debris. After seeing the big difference their efforts made, they went on to clean up a corner lot nearby, even adding a novelty trash can and some new trees. These experiences were a benefit and inspiration to others, as well as unforgettable ecology lessons.

BUILD SELF-FULFILLING SUCCESS IMAGES IN STUDENTS

The teachers who will long be remembered with gratitude and warmth are the ones who, like the A+ Teachers in our survey, have a high regard for learning—and an even higher regard for the learner! Our statistics show that although academics are important to outstanding educators one other goal is more important: developing positive self-images in students. These teachers realize that children who get acceptance and personal encouragement from their teachers will do better academically.

What do these award-winning teachers do to cement such positive bonds between themselves, their students, and the subject matter?

See that students get recognition

Gil Marshall, who teaches both junior and senior high school students in a Baltimore Experimental School, applies TLC (tender loving care) to all of his students to correct feelings of inadequacy regarding their learning abilities. He does this by speaking often with individuals and helping them to see their strong points.

Connie Anderson periodically plans an *"Everybody's a Winner Day"* to get students to see their positive attributes. At one point or another during the day, each student receives a ribbon of recognition for something he or she does well.

Brenda Pena finds that by treating students with *consideration* and dignity both attitudes and academics are elevated. This is borne out by a study of the relationship between teacher actions and student achievement which shows that frequent use of *thanks* to student responses results in greater subject knowledge.[2]

Lettie Siddens' students know that their best efforts will not go unnoticed, but will become part of colorful *bulletin board displays* acknowledging their individual achievements.

Rinna Wolfe's students know they are "somethin' special" when their teacher takes time to write them into *Mathematics story problems* and other classwork—and they seldom have trouble solving problems in which they are featured!

Kindergarten teacher Sharon A. Watson uses a *"strength-bombardment technique"* to improve student work. The children are taught to make accurate and constructive comments about each other's efforts, approaches, and products, such as "What I like about . . . is . . .," "It was a good idea to . . .," and so on. She has seen definite proof that this type of encouraging but unbiased peer appraisal helps the students to believe in themselves and their learning abilities.

Assure each child a certain degree of success

Rinna Wolfe of California stresses student success by using many assignments for which there is no right answer and in which all can succeed. These *"Every Kid Can Win"* activities include specially prepared lessons which utilize creative, divergent, and critical thinking; and they are generally followed by related activities with clay, paint, crayons, and other media.

To assure success, Gunnar Horn *breaks down tasks* to minute parts, if necessary, for his high school English students. He has also found that the way he approaches the situation and student can help or hinder the student's success. For example, comments like "Here's a hard one" rather than "Here's an easy one" or "I must have explained that unclearly" instead of "Didn't you listen?" go much farther in motivating students to try again until they finally succeed.

A *"Ladders of Success"* system had a very positive effect on the overall attitudes and achievement of my third-graders. This approach, which we used daily for a number of weeks, involved the students in drawing 6x2-inch ladders as shown in Exhibit 1-2. The rungs of the ladders represented subject areas, and the children could "climb" them by completing one of the applicable multi-level activities in each area. A ladder with six "successes" (marked by colorful stickers) earned a free-choice activity before a new ladder would offer more opportunities for continued success.

EXHIBIT 1-2: LADDERS OF SUCCESS

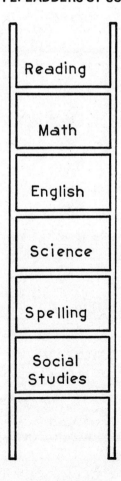

HELP STUDENTS BOOST THEIR EGOS AS WELL
AS THEIR GRADES

Positive recognition and success experiences will work wonders for student report cards, but A+ Teachers want more than just good grades for their students. They also want them to feel good about themselves, and so they encourage their students' creativity, talents, and individual interests. How do "those who do it best" suggest that we help our students to develop the kind of healthy self-perceptions which will enable them to find personal satisfaction and enjoyment in life?

Zero in on their unique assets

In Mark Thomashow's class, a *"Yellow Pages" resource book* was devised which itemizes student talents and areas of expertise, ranging from school subjects to skillful hobbies. Each student is listed several times and, according to Mr. Thomashow, it is an effective way to "accent the positive" and give everyone's ego a giant boost![3]

Maralene Wesner asks each of her students to supply her with information, pictures, stories, newspaper clippings, and other memorabilia about themselves for a special *"class diary"* she assembles and treasures.

Max Dicken enjoys using his own writing talents to create *"customized" plays* for his sixth-graders, seeing that each child has a part tailored to his or her special abilities, interests, or desires.

Gladys Oelkers draws a child's name from a special box each Monday to choose a *"Personality of the Week,"* who shares opinions, hobbies, and special interests with the class. The child is also given a prominent role in classroom activities that week.

"Being selected generates as much excitement as winning the lottery," observes Mrs. Oelkers. "The child is the all-important person for a week—and that 'rosy glow' lasts much longer."[4]

Put students in the giver's role

Sarah Schreiner does not worry about making mistakes in front of her kindergarteners because if she does make them, her students offer both sympathy and assistance. They have learned to be diplomatic *"mistake spotters,"* and, by helping others, they have realized that their own mistakes can also be stepping stones to learning.

In Roger Perkins' classroom, students opened a *"Santa's Repair Shop"* and fixed damaged toys to distribute to underprivileged children. In summarizing the activity, Mr. Perkins remarked that much incidental learning took place, but that the joy of giving had made the greatest impression on the children.[5]

High school students in Ann Nicoll's Health and Psychology classes learn a great deal about their subjects by becoming *community volunteers* for hospitals, institutions, education centers, counseling services, and the like. They also receive that special satisfaction of knowing that their help is both needed and appreciated.

When studying Latin America, students in Rinna Wolfe's class heard a news broadcast appealing for aid to Chile. The concerned fifth-graders responded by planning an *assistance campaign* for a needy Chilean community, collecting more than 8,000 pounds of seeds, shrubs, fertilizer, farm tools, medical supplies, soap, and CARE donations. They constructed a Spanish/English dictionary to send, traveled to hospitals for medical supplies, and wrote letters or spoke to noted people, large companies, and others who could help. They even earned much of the money themselves. Their reward? The way they felt about themselves afterwards!

"LET GO" AND PUT THE STUDENTS IN THE DRIVER'S SEAT!

Once you have made studies meaningful, set the stage for student success, and given students a good feeling about themselves, they are more than ready to take a good deal of their learning into their own hands. According to our survey, A+ Teachers recognize and meet their students' need for independence by giving them more opportunities to question and seek their own answers—by guiding them in the "hows" of learning as well as the "whats." You, too, can encourage this type of student initiative if you:

Offer exciting options

In Barbara Payne's junior high school, *special mini-courses* have met with astounding success. Students choose six-week courses several times a year from an amazing list which includes Leathercraft, Ceramics, Journalism, Boating and Fishing, Photography, Languages, Embroidery, First Aid, Square Dancing, and Birdwatching, to name a few.

Judith Sorrenti makes sure her elementary students have many *in-class choices*. For example, she often prepares lists of activities, any of which will fulfill requirements of an assignment. Exhibit 1-3 exemplifies a "choice list" for a book report assignment.

EXHIBIT 1-3: CHOICE LIST

1. Design a simple "roller movie" on shelf paper showing major events in the book. Use captions or "conversation bubbles."
2. Read an especially exciting chapter aloud to a friend. See if he or she can accurately predict the outcome of the book.
3. Make paper puppets and prepare a show about the book.
4. Pretend you are a newspaper reporter writing a review of the book for the newspaper.
5. Make an attractive book jacket; summarize the story on the "flaps."
6. Construct a crossword puzzle about people and events in the story.
7. Write a letter to the author and discuss the book.
8. Create a story of your own with the same title. How does it differ from the one you read?
9. Write a letter recommending the book to a friend.
10. Make a shoe-box diorama of a favorite scene. Write an explanatory description for interested viewers.
11. Dress as a character or object in the book and tell the story from his, her, or its point of view.
12. Create your own project to be discussed with the teacher.

A high school Metal Shop teacher, Hugh T. Lane, believes that his students reinforce their good feelings about themselves and develop initiative when they *design their own projects.* For example, if a student wants a frame for his aquarium at home, he plans in detail the size, specifications, and procedures he will follow in making it. Mr. Lane "checks out" plans during private conferences and is always available when assistance is needed. The rest, however, is up to the student. The result? Some very practical and well-made projects—and some very capable and confident students!

Give them some "eye-opening" responsibilities

Carol Thollander and a colleague, Leslie Kraus, devised a way of helping children to get to know themselves better (and thus to be more responsible and independent) by giving them the opportunity to express themselves in *"feelings notebooks."* Students use these notebooks to write about their thoughts and experiences. Their private entries are not corrected but can be voluntarily shared with teacher or class. Those needing some inspiration may select from a variety of "guide sheets" like the one in Exhibit 1-4. Very often a student will elaborate by adding an original story, poem, or illustration on the back before putting the page into his or her book.

EXHIBIT 1-4: "FEELINGS NOTEBOOK " GUIDE SHEET

Date_____

A good thing that happened to me today was

_____

_____

Something I didn't want to happen was

_____

_____

Something I wanted to do, but didn't was

_____

_____

I felt happy today when

_____

_____

Something I can do very well is

_____

_____

Alice Kihn's students are given a doubly responsible task when they are asked to complete the questionnaire in Exhibit 1-5, following a special class activity. They take a serious look at their emotions during the activity so that both they and their teacher gain insights for making their school experience more productive.

EXHIBIT 1-5: STUDENT FEELINGS SURVEY

Name _____ Date _____ Activity _____

1. During this activity,
   how did you feel about . . .

Excited 😆	Good 🙂	Bored 😕	No Feeling ⚪	Bad 🙁

   a) what you were doing?

   b) yourself?

   c) the teacher?

   d) your classmates?

2. How do you think your teacher felt about you? _____

3. How did you feel when you had to stop? _____

4. What part of this activity did you like best? _____

5. What part didn't you like? _____

6. If you could choose your own activity, what would it be? _____

12

Girolama Garner did some original research with his fifth- and sixth-graders by having them list types of talking and listening behavior. The students observed themselves during video-taped small-group lessons, coding and recording their behavior every ten seconds. Many were surprised to find that they twisted their hair, chewed on a pencil, or knew more than they thought they did. Students independently and individually decided what they liked about themselves and what, if anything, they wanted to change. They then assumed responsibility for reinforcing their desired behavior. Participating students improved significantly in both non-verbal behavior *and* self-concept—and they had done it all themselves![6]

* * * * * *

What kind of difference will *you* make in the lives of your students? Will you join ranks with the A+ Teachers who put their "hearts" into developing students who are not only knowledgeable, skillful, and well-behaved but also independent, creative, and self-confident?

Will you involve your students in current issues; will you capitalize upon individual talents and interests; will you help students to feel good about themselves? If so, you may well be counted among those highly regarded and long remembered teachers whose students learn not because they *have* to, but because they *want* to.

* * * * * *

2 HOW TO TAP THAT INEXHAUSTIBLE STREAM OF "SUPER" TEACHING IDEAS

Where do outstanding teachers get their ideas and inspirations? Are they just naturally more creative or gifted than others in the teaching profession, or are they more adept at locating and utilizing the best resources? A small group of elementary teachers is debating this very question as they informally discuss a highly respected colleague:

Teacher A: Did you stop in Walt's room lately? You've got to see his latest gadget. It's a mini "Math-o-Bike." This one tops them all! The kids get to sit on a real mini-bike for imaginary trips—and end up gladly doing a host of practical mathematical calculations!

Teacher B: He's always bubbling over with new approaches and fresh perspectives! Wasn't that assembly program his class presented last week absolutely sensational?

Teacher C: And remember that "Teacher Sharing Program" he talked us all into last year? I'm still using some of the good ideas I got from it.

Teacher D: Where does he get all his fantastic ideas? I also like to try new things every so often, but I can't compare to Walt. Guess my mind just isn't as fertile as his.

Teacher A: I know what you mean, but we needn't feel badly. Walt is just one of those unusually gifted people. We're not even in his "league."

Teacher C: Gifted? Maybe. But I say that Walt's exceptional accomplishments are *not* the result of some Divine endowment. Haven't you noticed that he's always actively searching for new ideas and methods? Last semester he took that "Innovations" course, remember? And this semester he's attending the Math seminar at the Teachers' Center.

14

Teacher B: That's right. And he seldom sits around just chatting. He's usually leafing through those educational magazines, engrossed in one of Glasser's books, or maybe checking something in the curriculum guide.

Teacher C: He also takes professional days to visit outstanding teachers and new programs. Why, he even asked me if he could sit in on my class during his free period to get ideas!

Teacher A: I guess you're right. He certainly *is* creative, but many of his ideas do come from other sources—even from his students! It can't be that his students are so much more capable; it has to be that he gives them more opportunities to express their own ideas and offer suggestions. And they sure come through with "winners" for him!

Teacher D: Excuse me, Phyllis. I don't mean to interrupt, but would you please hand me that copy of *Instructor?*

According to our in-depth survey of more than 400 contemporary educators, those who excel are distinguished not because they rely a great deal more on their own ideas, but because they get more ideas from a wider variety of sources.

This chapter will show how you, like the A+ Teachers in our survey, can get many good teaching ideas by:
- benefiting from others' knowledge and experiences through books and periodicals,
- taking advantage of educational seminars and other professional opportunities,
- making the curriculum guide an effective teaching aid,
- looking to other teachers for ideas and assistance, and
- "picking the minds" of those who have so much at stake, the students themselves!

As you read about the A+ Teachers' relentless search for ways to make teaching and learning more satisfying, you are likely to find some new ways to:

DISCOVER PRICELESS "GEMS" IN EDUCATIONAL AND OTHER MEDIA

What *educational periodicals* do you read? Top-rated teachers—especially those holding bachelor degrees, having at least twenty years of experience, and working in inner-city environments—are avid readers of the most popular teacher magazines. The professional publication with the largest readership from both groups of teachers is *Today's Education,* which is put out by the National Education Association for teachers at all grade levels.

The ones *read significantly more* by A+ Teachers than by Other Teachers are these readable, action-packed, and relevant resources:

- *Instructor,* a periodical for teachers and supervisors through grade eight,
- *Learning,* a magazine for elementary teachers,
- *Changing Education,* a quarterly journal of the American Federation of Teachers, for educators at all grade levels and in all subjects, now available only as a supplement to the monthly *American Teacher,* and
- *Teacher,* formerly *Grade Teacher,* an aid to teachers at kindergarten through junior high school levels.

In addition to reading more educational periodicals more often, A+ Teachers find additional ideas in over 120 *other magazines.* Those cited most often were *Early Years,* state education association magazines, *The English Journal, Reading Teacher, Math Teacher, Phi Delta Kappan,* and *Media and Method.*

Others mentioned included general magazines such as *Time, Saturday Review, Ebony Junior, Newsweek,* and *National Geographic,* or magazines related to a specific subject, for example, *School Shop, Instrumentalist, Science Teacher,* or *Arts and Activities.*

Books, too, can help you to "keep up" with the latest educational developments, to find successful teaching strategies, and to enrich yourself professionally. A+ Teachers tap this resource regularly.

Has any one book had a major influence on your teaching? When participating teachers were asked this question a galaxy of titles filled the air! The ones cited most often, and, interestingly, *only* by A+ Teachers, were first the Bible and then *Schools Without Failure* by William Glasser.

The Bible was credited for being a major factor in shaping attitudes and actions on and off the job, and *Schools Without Failure* was unanimously regarded as a practical guide for making school the joyful, productive, and successful experience it can and should be for most students. The book holding third place, noted by several from both groups, was Sylvia Ashton-Warner's classic, *Teacher.*

Listed by more than one teacher were the following:

Teaching as a Subversive Activity (Postman)
The Come-Alive Classroom (Cook, Caldwell, Christiansen)
Dare to Discipline (Dobson)
Future Shock (Toffler)
Problems in Reading (Dolch)
Reality Therapy (Glasser)
Between Teacher and Child (Ginott)
Crisis in the Classroom (Silberman)
Death at an Early Age (Kozol)
Increase Reading Ability (Harris)
Diagnosis and Correction (Bond and Tinker)
How Children Fail (Holt)
Summerhill (Neill)

Also mentioned were educational books like *Discover Your Teaching Self, Open Education,* and *Freedom to Learn,* inspirational books like *The Miracle Worker, The Power of Positive Thinking,* and *I'm OK, You're OK,* and books relating to specialized fields such as *Encounter with Anthropology* and *Has Market Capitalism Collapsed?*

Some teachers praised educators and authors like Piaget and Holt for their influence rather than identifying a specific book; others cited biographies of great people like Thomas Jefferson and George Washington Carver. One teacher noted a practical activity book she and some colleagues devised during a teaching workshop, and others submitted their own original titles like *The Book of Experience* and *My Own Book of Life* representing that "best seller" in each of us!

Our obvious conclusion is that the letters R-E-A-D have a special meaning for teachers: Reach — Explore — Apply — Discover! Yes, the written word will always be a beacon to the enthusiastic and striving educator.

OBTAIN VALUABLE INPUT THROUGH COURSES AND WORKSHOPS

There are a myriad of ever-changing workshops, courses, and seminars in response to current educational needs and desires. If you wish to extend your knowledge, pick up practical "pointers," find new ideas and approaches, or seek overall improvement, there is a wide selection of conventions, educational fairs and conferences, in-service courses, and even excellent, accredited, televised graduate courses available. According to statistical results of our survey, this is an area in which the "super successful" teachers are much more involved.

John M. Selig spends his summers in *Math and Computer Institutes* and also tries to find a Math-related summer job. Working for NASA and the U.S. Army, for example, has helped him to make Mathematics an exciting and relevant subject for his upper-grade students.

A teacher of high school Business Educaton in Illinois credits his ever-changing approaches and materials to ideas gained by attending *conferences* and college courses frequently; Alex Dobrowolski considers five NSF Institutes to have made "a great contribution to my teaching."

Helen B. Guptill attended a *course* entitled "Innovative Methods," in which she learned about a teaching approach she has found to be extremely successful with her eighth-grade Science students. Another teacher, Sharon A. Watson, has been a part of a *training program* at the Institute for Staff Development in Miami, Florida. She is now a leader and instructor in a specialized approach, called BASICS, which helps pre-school, elementary, and special education students to develop fundamental thinking skills.

MAKE THE CURRICULUM GUIDE WORK FOR YOU

When is the last time you took a good, thorough look at the curriculum guide for your course or grade level? If you cannot recall, perhaps it is time to see what assistance it can offer! The A+ Teachers in our survey tended toward a more moderate reliance on the curriculum guide, referring to it periodically for ideas and guidance in contrast to the more extreme practices of Other Teachers, who tended to almost ignore it or to depend upon it too much.

Do not underestimate the value of this aid! Some of the most highly acclaimed teachers confided that a formal curricular outline had been a great educational influence. An Auto Mechanics curriculum guide, a kindergarten guide for a particular locality, and state guidelines were cited specifically as the "books" which had been most helpful. Also commended were commercial series like the "James Moffet Student-Centered Language Arts Curriculum" and the "Earth Science Curriculum Project."

Other A+ Teachers had found their curriculum guides to be less inspiring, and decided to do something about it. Carolyn C. Haines and a colleague created their own *"Course of Studies,"* which outlines the entire first grade experience—and Maralene Wesner co-authored a *kindergarten curriculum*, which is now commercially available.[1] Other teachers have made similar efforts:

- High school teacher Mario Fierros developed a *"Foreign Language Curriculum Guide"* for teachers of modern languages in his school district. It includes course descriptions, performance objectives, suggested teaching methods, and learning activities. Mr. Fierros studied seven curriculum guides in six different states before compiling and creating what he considered to be right for his school system.

- Harry H. Koch of Illinois felt the need for teachers to be prepared for the metric system and designed courses of study entitled *"Unifield Mathematics and Metrics"* for use in his high school.

- Moke C. Owens devised a kindergarten through grade 12 curriculum for a required course in *Humanities*, which encompasses "space arts" (painting, sculpture, and architecture), "time arts" (music, poetry, and literature) and "time-space arts" (theatre, dance, and opera). This curriculum received positive feedback from parents, teachers, *and* students.

- Shirley A. Johnson has given many hours and much of her expertise to develop a *"Science Curriculum"* for her community. It contains subject matter and "tested" lessons for students from grades 1 through 12. It purposely exposes students to each topic more than once, at different grade levels.

HAVE ABLE COLLEAGUES SERVE AS YOUR CONSULTANTS!

A study of 312 teachers with less than three years of experience showed that their greatest help came from veteran teachers with whom they worked.[2] Looking to other educators also proved to be a distinguishing characteristic of the A+ Teachers in our sampling.

How can educators support and encourage one another? Consider the following:

- Eva Korth, a New Jersey elementary teacher, has been so successful with her "open classroom" approaches that she offers *workshops* each year to spread the concepts and to help teachers learn the practicalities of this type of set-up.

- Lee Oberparleiter has found many workable solutions to teacher dilemmas through his own study and experience. He passes his learning along, and gets teachers to seek their own answers by giving very timely *extension courses* on "Matching Teaching and Learning Styles," "Conflict and Resolutions," "Humanizing Your Classroom," and other topics that "hit home."[3]

- Jean D'Arcy Maculaitis often holds *informal seminars* in her own living room. Advice, information, and helpful materials are shared with teachers of foreign-born students, like herself.

- Bank Street School in New York City has weekly *staff exchanges* during which teachers discuss what they are doing in class. Good ideas, on-going projects, and successful approaches—as well as problems—are brought up. The teachers report that they (and their students!) benefit greatly.

- Elementary teachers in River Vale, N.J., have two different but equally valuable *sharing sessions* each month. The first are gatherings of representatives from each grade level to discuss a particular subject (one group focuses on reading, another on math, etc.) and the second are meetings of teachers at the same grade level—to discuss outcomes of the first meetings.

You can get some helpful "peer assistance" by joining *special organizations* like "Teacher Works in a Box," which offers teachers semi-annual "goodies boxes" containing ideas and successful lessons used by fellow members.[4] A similar organization, "Zephros," sends its members books, posters, newsletters, workbooks, and other teaching materials which are secured at reduced prices.[5]

Other good possibilities include visiting *outstanding educational programs* (often described in booklets available through state departments of education) and *observing exceptional teachers*. Ruth Elwell, a kindergarten teacher in Nebraska, credits Project Head Start for giving her useful ideas; the "Right to Read" program has inspired Josephine J. Owen, a junior high school teacher, to try some new and very effective teaching methods; and Diane Mazzei was so enthused when she visited a great teacher who was using a learning center approach that she tried it too—with striking results!

GAIN A GOLDMINE OF "BRIGHT IDEAS" FROM THAT OFTEN OVERLOOKED RESOURCE—YOUR STUDENTS!

What is the most important fact to remember when comparing the resources tapped by A+ Teachers with those used by Other Teachers? It is that A+ Teachers look to their own students for ideas and inspiration more often! Yes, this "backyard goldmine" is so obvious that we frequently overlook it. But why *not* seek assistance from the very ones for whom the entire education system is functioning?! The greater use of this "natural resource" by the better teachers contributes substantially to their success.

When Lola Lehman, the director in a school-wide learning center, notices that materials leave a void or gap, as they often do, she encourages her students to present ideas, solutions, and *student-made materials* to fill it. "The results are not necessarily unique, but they are truly helpful to both teacher and student," says Ms. Lehman.

Kindergarten teacher Sharon A. Watson uses the traditional *"Show and Tell" activity* to trigger student ideas and interests—and when a spark is ignited, she fuels it. One student, for example, brought in three plastic dinosaurs which he had put together at home. An intrigued class went on to read and write stories, visit the museum, construct a papier-mâche' dinosaur from a large box, and present an original play to which parents were invited.

Carl R. Berg, a fourth-grade teacher, had his students pursue their idea of making *"houses"* out of their desks using a variety of ideas and materials to make it a private learning area. According to Mr. Berg, the enthusiastic students actually did better academically when the "houses" were completed and used. The students took an interest in consumer education, which was further encouraged when they bought and sold their "houses" at current market prices. What the buying and selling led to is anybody's guess, but one can be sure that their teacher was there observing, listening, and ready to capitalize upon student ideas and interests!

Fifth-graders in Marie Hanlon's class took a variety of trips to nearby historical sites to coincide with the Bicentennial celebration. When one student had the clever idea to transform the notes he took during these trips into an interesting tourist book, Ms. Hanlon encouraged him to do so. The resulting *student-created guide* entitled "Just a Stone's Throw" was published and distributed locally during the Bicentennial year!

For a change of pace, I encouraged my third-graders to make *independent investigations* of self-selected topics. Students liked it so much that it became an on-going activity. A surprisingly diverse selection of topics surfaced—and it was a thrill to see the knowledge gained, the enthusiasm generated, and the respect that grew among the students as they helped each other locate magazines, pictures, books, and anything else that might relate to the chosen topics.

Many exciting activities evolved from these independent studies. One girl's interest in nursing led to a class tour of the local hospital; she helped to make the arrangements and to prepare the class for the trip. Another girl's interest in modeling led to "Miss Joy's Boutique Fashion Show" in which both male and female "creations" were displayed for an all-school assembly program. A boy's love of animals brought to us a speaker, a film, and a live animal from the "Lost Pet Association." Interest in handicrafts resulted in parents displaying skills like sewing and smocking . . . and so on . . . and so on. All participated, and it was, indeed, a very rich year for all of us.

Lee Oberparleiter of New Jersey tells how students in his alternative high school *brainstorm ideas* for topics they would like to study. Students assist the faculty by suggesting activities, trips, and books to read, and even by helping to set up time schedules for classes. Mr. Oberparleiter reports that, although most of the time students ask for traditional courses and activities, they sometimes come up with fascinating new ones.

*   *   *   *   *   *

Why do the most effective educators seem to overflow with electrifying ideas? Because their minds are "working overtime," incessantly speculating: "Is there anything of interest here for my students . . . and how can I use this in my teaching?"

They draw not only from books, periodicals, workshops, the curriculum guide, and colleagues, but also from unexpected sources: their own former teachers, retired teachers, student teachers, friends, spouses, *and* their own students. They see the seasons, the needs of the local community, and even department stores' decorative themes as "idea instigators." One teacher looks to her personal travel experiences, another reflects while walking home each day, and a third claims to find ideas "just about everywhere."

It is this openness and constant searching which can lead us to that inexhaustible stream of "super" teaching ideas, just waiting to be tapped!

*   *   *   *   *   *

3 SIMPLIFIED PLANNING PROCEDURES YOU WILL FIND BOTH PRACTICAL AND EFFICIENT

Planning ahead is one of the most important skills a teacher must master. Why? Because efficient plans are vital to the kind of day-to-day teaching that results in sound, substantial student learning.

Let's listen to the breakfast conversation of an experienced substitute teacher. The topic of the discussion with her spouse is her current assignment to a high school Science class.

Substitute: This is the best substituting job I've ever had. It's really a delight!

Spouse: What makes this one different from others?

Sub: Well, that's hard to say. The teachers are friendly, the students are cooperative, and the room is well equipped . . . but I especially like the exceptional plans this teacher left for me.

Spouse: What do you mean? Can plans make such a difference?

Sub: You bet they can! For example, there's a chart posted near the teacher's desk with an overview of the entire six-week unit the classes are pursuing. I can see at a glance what each class has been doing, where it stands now, and where it is headed. This is really helpful because the plans differ from class to class. Each group took-part in making their own plans—and wow! These kids have some great ideas!

Spouse: Does that chart tell you exactly what to teach?

Sub: No, it's just an outline of questions and suggested activities. The daily plans are kept in a loose-leaf notebook, on forms the teacher devised. It's so much better than cramming them into the tiny boxes of the usual planbook.

Spouse: Do you *have* to follow the plans precisely? Can't you use your own ideas?

Sub: I don't hesitate to "do my own thing" because I get a distinct feeling that this teacher mainly cares about the students—that they have a productive day, either following his plans *or* mine. In fact, listen to this little piece of advice he has posted on the cover of his planbook for substitutes:

> "This planbook should not be a dictator—
> Just a helpful resource or guide.
> So, if something better beckons,
> Then please, lay these plans aside."

Spouse: A remarkable teacher!

Sub: Sorry, I have to rush off, Darling. I *really* don't want to be late. Bye, bye (throws kiss) . . . and have a good day!

Spouse: See you later, Hon. I'd wish you a good day too, but I already know you'll have one!

This chapter will show you how A+ Teachers develop efficient planning systems by:

- devising effective long-range plans,
- preparing exciting and creative short-range plans,
- leaving room for those extraordinary spur-of-the-moment teaching opportunities,
- drawing students into the planning, and
- making the most productive use of both time and ingenuity.

How do you plan and prepare yourself to face the daily teaching challenge? This is one of the key questions in our survey. Over 400 educators responded. The practices and recommendations of the most successful ones add up to a "practical planning guide" which can help you to:

SET YOUR SIGHTS FOR THE ESSENTIALS WITH LONG-RANGE PLANNING

How can a teacher make sure that the class does not "whittle away" precious time, and that all-important objectives are sufficiently stressed? According to Edward E. Bowman, *larger, more ambitious goals* are the answer. His long-range planning helps him avoid meaningless "fillers" which waste student time, and it also enables him to use his daily and weekly planning periods more effectively.

Charles C. Noble said, "You must have long-range goals to keep from being frustrated by short-range failures." A+ Teachers appear to agree with both of these gentlemen; our survey shows that they are more likely to make plans which project at least a month ahead. High school teachers, especially, favor this type of planning.

Sheryl Hinman writes out her long-range plans in terms of the *accomplishments* she expects from her junior high school English students. In Speech, for example, a listing of major activities (giving a speech, presenting an original drama, taking part in a debate, appearing on video tape, etc.) provides her focal points for more detailed planning.

The Come-Alive Classroom, a popular teacher idea book written by twenty master teachers, recommends the use of white shelf paper to plot out the entire *year at a glance.* Content to be covered, major concepts to be learned, skills to be taught, resources to be used, and even activities to "make it all happen" are listed.[1] This large mural-like chart can then be posted in the classroom as a valuable guide for teacher planning and a constant invitation to students to contribute their ideas.

Carolyn C. Haines and Constance Tartaglione make a yearly overview in the form of an attractive *parent booklet* outlining the program which will be tailored to their first-graders. It describes, subject by subject, what will be taught and what materials will be used. This special "Course of Studies" is not only the teachers' master plan but it also encourages parents to take a more active role in their children's education.

TAKING THE DRUDGERY OUT OF SHORT-RANGE PLANNING

A+ Teachers are far less likely to use the traditional lined or boxed commercial planbook—apparently because they want more flexibility *and* space. If they do use it for listing highlights, they often supplement it with a variety of original planning tools.

Wally Bain, for example, uses special *daily plan sheets* of his own design—like the one in Exhibit 3-1—to outline his high school Science lessons. He does not always stick to these "scripts," but he credits them for much of the success of his smooth-running classes.

Angela Folli also uses her own format to meet her particular planning needs. Her mimeographed *weekly schedules* contain all the "fixed" routines (Music class, milk money collections, recess time, and the like) and plenty of empty space for writing in activities that

EXHIBIT 3-1: DAILY PLAN SHEET

CLASS _____	DATE _____
UNIT _____	TOPIC _____

BEHAVIORAL OBJECTIVE(S) _____
_____
_____

TIME ALLOTMENT	ACTIVITIES

ASSIGNMENT

MATERIALS	REFERENCES

do change. Thus, she spends less time on repetitious entries and more time where it counts.

Margaret Simpson needs a *flexible planbook* for her combination second- and third-grade class; so she makes her own. She sections off boxes in a regular, lined composition notebook, organizing her written notes in a variety of ways. Because her students are working at three different levels in Language Arts, for example, she has three sets of plans for this subject. These are recorded in three separate columns of boxes on the same page to give her an "overall picture" of all three groups while she is working with any one of them.

Donna Floreen, who visits several classes a day teaching Music to elementary and junior high school students, uses her own *planning charts,* as shown in Exhibit 3-2. These help her to plan a "balanced" musical experience for each group and serve, also, as record-keeping aids. She adds notes and evaluations during and after each class to help her answer questions like these when preparing the next week's forms:

- Where did we leave off?
- What went well? Were there any problems?
- What special student interests can be further pursued?
- How could last week's lesson have been improved?

EXHIBIT 3-2: WEEKLY PLAN SHEET

Class: _____ Week of: _____		
Musical Theory	Music Appreciation	Singing

Chances are that you would never find Lily DeCleir's head "buried" in a planbook at the wrong time, because she puts important guidelines on *display charts* for quick and easy reference during lessons. A permanent one, for example, hangs in the Reading corner as a reminder for her to:

- review applicable phonetic rules as new words are decoded by students,
- ask questions to check comprehension, and provide experience in scanning, pinpointing the main idea, drawing conclusions, interpreting, and so on,
- give students practice in both silent and oral reading,
- discuss authors, story purpose, student ideas, etc.

For teachers like these, planning is a challenging, on-going endeavor which lays a firm academic basis, eliminates wasted time and energy, and helps to bring forth one's greatest teaching self. It is anything *but* drudgery!

LET YOUR PLANS GO PRODUCTIVELY AMISS

Although A+ Teachers put much of themselves into their plans, they are more ready to abandon them for unanticipated journeys. Sharon A. Watson, for example, often lets her observant and enthusiastic students lead her into exciting and *unexpected areas of study*. Snowflakes sticking to the jackets of her primary students led to an in-depth investigation of snowflakes—and a host of related "spin-offs" like the water cycle, animals in winter, winter sports, and different climates.

A spontaneous walk after an ice storm was followed by an unscheduled discussion for Brenda Pena's intrigued students, and Mary M. Harris laid her plans aside one day when students noticed a nearby *building being demolished*. The entire class, in awe of the proceedings, was soon deliberating about the machinery, noise, dust, the former inhabitants, and what might replace the building. The students never saw the film Ms. Harris had planned to show, but what they saw was better: a real-life drama![2]

How and when should you give rein to sudden, unplanned activities? The better prepared you are, the more choices are open to you. Your decision will depend upon the depth of student interest and the range of educational possibilities in a particular diversion. If all systems are "go," and you have some leeway built into your long-range plans, then why not give whole-hearted pursuit?

ENLIST STUDENTS AS CO-PLANNERS

A distinguishing characteristic of A+ Teachers is their ability to get students more actively involved in planning.

Does this involvement make a difference? To find out, one researcher divided fourth- and fifth-graders into two groups. One group helped to devise its own study plan along with the teacher, and the other group followed a prescribed program. Afterwards, academic achievement and attitudes were compared. Both groups gained the required knowledge, but the co-planners evidenced a greater liking for the subject—and a preference for that way of learning![3]

Two upper-grade teachers, Ann Nicoll and Don Gibson, allow their students to *set weekly goals.* Ms. Nicoll's class helps in making a projective outline of the week's work, and later in reviewing the results. Mr. Gibson's students meet with him individually to plan customized weekly programs based on the previous week's accomplishments. Students receive a "check" for goals attained, a "plus" for goals exceeded, and a "minus" for goals unmet.

Rinna Wolfe's students sometimes *plan lessons* individually or in small groups. Materials are gathered and teaching approaches planned. At other times her students work as tutors, watching her teach a lesson, then using similar methods for helping classmates who were absent or need extra assistance.

Students in Eva Korth's class *prepare daily schedules,* including requirements, special lessons with the teacher, and activities of their choice. At the end of the day, quality and quantity are evaluated. Exhibit 3-3 shows one type of schedule which Mrs. Korth's students have used.

You may even try giving students the opportunity to plan a project or long-range study and to *select their own grade* for accomplishing it. Mary Ann Brady did this with great success. Each of her junior high school students made a "plan of action" to meet specified, but varied, requirements for the mark he or she desired.

Finally, students can *provide input for teacher planning.* Romaine Beideleman's primary students get a chance to record their suggestions on a cassette recorder, which is always set up in a corner of the classroom. Her students can't complain that they never get to do anything they like, because their ideas are used for the following month's plans.[4]

EXHIBIT 3-3: STUDENT PLANNING FORM

Name: _____   Date: _____

SCHEDULE

Monday	Tuesday	Wednesday	Thursday	Friday

Completed?
Yes___ No___   Yes___ No___   Yes___ No___   Yes___ No___   Yes___ No___

Quality Rating:

Great ___	Great ___	Great ___	Great ___	Great ___
Good ___	Good ___	Good ___	Good ___	Good ___
Fair ___	Fair ___	Fair ___	Fair ___	Fair ___
Poor ___	Poor ___	Poor ___	Poor ___	Poor ___

Students can also help teachers develop listings, study guides, or flow charts like the one in Exhibit 3-4. Here students and teacher together have set forth sub-topics for their study of water. The students can assist further by adding activities and factual material to this framework.[5]

EXHIBIT 3-4: TEACHER- AND CLASS-DESIGNED FLOWCHART

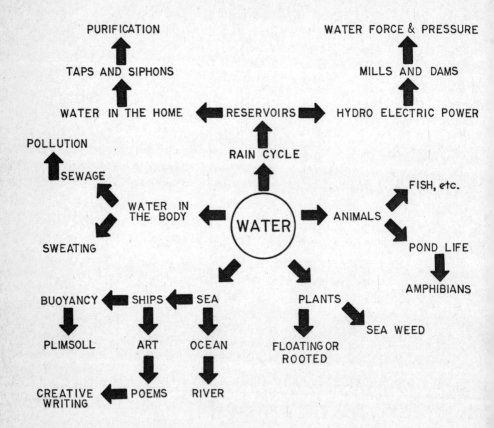

RISE FROM BEING DISORGANIZED TO BECOMING A "SUPER PLANNER"!

What are the prerequisites to good planning? A look at the experiences and practices of A+ Teachers leads us to believe that one should . . .

Have students in mind when planning

Questions like these may point the way during the planning process:

1. What are the real needs of my students? How can I meet these with (or along with) what I plan to teach?
2. What current student interests can be used as motivators?
3. Who may find this too easy? Who may be frustrated by it? How can I build in "safeguards" for these students?
4. Can I include activities to elicit student creativity? . . . independent initiative? . . . enthusiasm?

One high school teacher, Mrs. Jett Campbell, believes so strongly in *fitting the curricula to the students* that she seldom uses the same plans again. She would rather scrap last year's successful plans and work out new ones than not meet the unique needs of a student or class.

Be organized

Teachers who have "made the grade" suggest the following:

1. Have long-range goals in mind so your plans will be on target.
2. Be prepared. Get materials ready ahead of time. Always have guidelines and plans available for substitutes.
3. Be expert in the subject matter, but still have plenty of references handy for those "stumpers" which students inevitably ask.
4. Build in "leeway" so you can take extra time if you need it—and productively use extra time if you have it.

A 5x8-inch file helps Janet L. Ryan organize a wealth of good ideas that save valuable planning time. Whenever she discovers or creates interesting activities, she summarizes them on individual cards and files them by subject.

Emily Pritchard Carey and Margaret Simpson do some *advanced planning* in order to be better organized during the school year. Ms. Carey uses her summer recess time to make special classroom aids, and Ms. Simpson fills out requests for films and materials far ahead of time so she'll be assured of getting them—and so she can put her time and talents to better uses during the busy school year.

Be original

Your plans will have more practical value if they are "right" for you. In order to make them so, you may have to:

1. Design a planning form unique to your needs.
2. Note ideas, activities, and lessons which are "hits," and try adapting subsequent ones to similar formats.
3. Be patient. Not all good ideas are flashes of inspiration. Sometimes they need time to develop and grow.
4. Use your own ingenuity and past experience for new slants, factual data, and teaching strategies.

Rinna Wolfe, a former department store buyer, views her students as "customers," herself as a "salesperson," and education as her "product." Not surprisingly, she abounds with originality as she constantly strives to turn out "satisfied customers"!

Plan with others

In addition to tapping that gold mine between your own ears, it would be to your advantage to also pick the brains of others. You may, for example, want to consider:

1. Planning sessions with colleagues, student teachers, volunteers, parents, substitutes, and others who take an interest in your students.
2. Principal assistance as a resource. Whether or not the principal routinely checks your plans, he or she may be delighted to be asked for additional suggestions.
3. Advice from in-school specialists, outside experts in a subject, people with study-related avocations, etc.
4. Opinions and pointers from objective educators, lay people, or even your own students as they review plans or observe you "in action."

Many schools arrange schedules so teachers of a grade or subject can meet together for *planning periods*. One high school in Ohio has set aside "planning days" during which teachers of a subject are freed from classes so they can get together to discuss and evaluate their plans.[6]

Plan for yourself

When making your plans, be sure to include some "hard thinking" about your own professional and personal growth.

1. Decide which educational periodicals you should subscribe to and read regularly.

2. Search for books, seminars, and other opportunities to expand your knowledge, increase your competence, or fill a need.

3. Look for weaknesses you should overcome, changes or improvements you'd like to make, and so on. Then make some practical plans for achieving these goals.

4. Finally, plan to "get away from it all" once in awhile. Pursue a new interest or hobby, take a much-desired vacation, etc. This will give you renewed vigor for teaching, make you a more fascinating person, and help you to avoid an overwork problem called "teacher burnout."[7]

* * * * * *

What, then, appears to be the essence of effective planning? One A+ Teacher sums it up for us: "You need efficient long-range plans to chart the course, and exciting short-range plans to make the journey."

Add to this more confidence in your own planning ability and less reliance on the prescribed "planbook" set-up, more student involvement, *and* a willingness to deviate from your "script" when a more promising avenue presents itself . . . and you will be a teacher well prepared to meet the challenges and appreciate the joys of your profession.

* * * * * *

4 THE ART OF TURNING A DRAB CLASSROOM INTO AN EXCITING STAGE FOR LEARNING

Does the physical environment in which a child learns have a significant impact on the quality of that learning?

It can certainly make a difference, according to the observations of one college student who visited an elementary classroom and made the following entry in his log:

I opened the door and was immediately aware of a warmth, a cheeriness, and a buzz of student activity. I got the distinct feeling that, here, children are the top priority and learning is both a joy and a privilege.

I began to analyze what had given me these strong impressions so soon. It might have been the colorful display of student-made folders which adorned a giant bulletin board. The attractive covers had titles such as "Horses," "Dragonflies," "Whales," etc., and inside were carefully researched facts, detailed illustrations, and creative stories. A nearby pouch contained duplicated lists of questions and activities which enticed the children to use these references.

Another display I couldn't resist exploring was called "Solve the Problem and Help Mickey Escape." A little mouse cut-out was being pursued by a cardboard cat. Students went to this exhibit to work on problems related to their current studies: math challenges, spelling quizzes, fill-ins, matching games, story finishing, and so on. For each task correctly completed, the student could move the mouse forward, but alas! Wrong answers progressed the cat! A little box of index cards next to this table invited the children to create their own problems, many of which could later be added to the display.

In addition there was a Social Studies area with a hand-sewn Colonial flag, models of the era, and task cards with independent student activities . . . and a learning center (with a poster above it saying "Just Write for the Occasion") which gave students the opportunity to create their own invitations, letters, stories, poems, brochures, progress notes to parents, puppet shows, TV commercials, etc.

The student desks were arranged in "clusters" rather than formal rows— and two students tenderly ministered to the needs of a gerbil family in a comfortable corner of the room. These observations further contributed to the "good vibrations" I was receiving.

Although the room was not the epitome of neatness that mine had been when I was in elementary school, it had a special aura about it which drew the children into active learning—and made me wish I could be nine years old again!

Yes, classroom set-up is one part of teaching that "the best in the league" never fail to consider—because of both the obvious and the subtle effects that the physical environment can have on student learning.

This chapter will show how you can make your classroom "some-place special" by:

- bringing in live animals,
- arranging and re-arranging your classroom for optimum learning,
- highlighting studies with displays and exhibits,
- making learning attractive with a "center approach," and
- trying something original with the room itself.

When A+ Teachers were asked to describe their classrooms, some significant facts were brought to light. Their rooms, in contrast to those of Other Teachers, reflected greater imagination and child-appeal. Yours, too, can be more exciting if you:

ADD " LIFE" TO YOUR CLASSROOM

Are students and teachers the only "life" in America's classrooms? Not at all! A good percentage of classrooms across the country contain additional forms of life. Plants, which have both aesthetic and educational value, are popular with teachers—and it is not unusual to find one or more *animals* "in residence."

A+ Teachers are more moderate in regard to live animals, being less likely than Other Teachers to always have them and even less likely to never have them. Elementary teachers, whose students have much to give and gain from classroom pets, proved to be ardent promoters of this type of classroom "guest." And inner-city teachers, whose students see fewer animals in their everyday lives, also tended to highly favor first-hand experiences with animals.

Tadpoles, gerbils, and guinea pigs are popular classroom additions, offering exciting opportunities for students to observe birth and growth, and of course *egg-hatching* is also a thrill for young and old alike!

Estrela Lopez recommends *parakeets* because of the great help they have been in encouraging her kindergarteners to verbalize and converse. Shirley Moore endorses the *ant farm,* which her class found intriguing—and *fish,* which motivated a variety of creative writing experiences for her students.

Richard Kaliszewski's *animal learning center* helped to develop his students' interest in reading—and much more! Each student was assigned a particular animal in the center for special study: a gerbil, a fish, a hamster, a garden snake, a turtle, etc. The children learned a great deal through formal lessons, demonstrations, books, filmstrips, and by keeping "life logs" about and actually caring for their animals.[1]

Martin J. Gutnik utilizes an 8x15x6-foot glass tank as a *giant terrarium* for his Science classes. A 3-foot deep lake, a stream, several waterfalls, marshland, and rocky highlands provide a natural environment for fish, snails, frogs, worms, salamanders, and fruit flies. His sixth-graders study reproduction, food chains, life cycles, and pollution through this fascinating display—and become "experts" and tour guides for other classes that visit.[2]

One teacher tells of her school's rule against certain animals, explaining that an animal bite has caused many problems and that communicable diseases must also be considered. For those who decide to use them, however, the pros can outweigh the cons if *careful thought and preparation* are given to their inclusion. I can personally attest to the fact that haphazard planning *can* be disastrous.

A well-intentioned student brought a cat to our classroom one afternoon. It was shown, discussed, and petted by all, but soon presented us with a problem: where to put it. He kept jumping out of his box, yet when left to roam at will, he became an "attractive nuisance." After a few fruitless attempts to keep him in the box, a student tried the opposite approach—putting the box on top of the cat. Our problem was solved; we no longer had a cat walking around the room. However, we *did* have a *box* walking around the room!

CREATE THE LEARNING ENVIRONMENT YOU WANT WITH THE FURNITURE YOU HAVE

Another important practice among teachers who excel is a more *flexible arrangement* of their furniture and learning materials. They are less likely to adhere to one set formation, especially regarding student desks. Twice as many Other Teachers, however, stick solely to the traditional desks-in-rows set-up.

Connie Anderson "gives" her room to the students, encouraging them to sit where they wish, either singly or in groups. Brenda Pena often puts students who work well together into pairs, changing partners periodically. Lois K. Smith switches student desk set-ups monthly and *changes* the total environment of the classroom almost as often.

Lettie Siddens seeks an atmosphere of warmth and homeyness for her primary students—and achieves it with a *circular arrangement* of students and a rocking chair for herself. Exhibit 4-1 diagrams this for you—and shows the many other little "touches" which make her room the joyful "learning laboratory" she wants it to be.

Lily DeCleir's room has *student rocking chairs* as well! When her second-graders come to the reading circle for their small-group lessons, they find child-size rockers—and an enjoyment in reading which is easily carried over to after-school hours. Exhibit 4-2 shows the reading circle and the clever uses to which Ms. DeCleir has put the existing space and materials.

Clusters of two to eight desks are practical for conserving space and for encouraging student communication or group work. Exhibit 4-3 shows desk patterns which two outstanding teachers highly recommend.

By *keeping a goal in mind,* a teacher can work wonders, even with the most depressing room. Take for example Jean D'Arcy Maculaitis. She was horrified when she first saw the old, dilapidated room in which she was to teach her junior and senior high school students. She very wisely channeled her negative emotions into creative and productive efforts, focusing on what she intended that room to be! She designed curtains, did some painting, planned

EXHIBIT 4-1: ELEMENTARY CLASSROOM

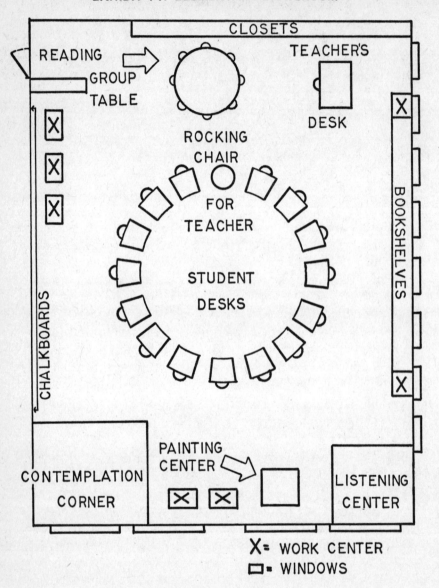

attractive displays, and did lots of re-arranging. Her fortunate students entered a bright, colorful room that September—one which radiated very positive feelings that the students also adopted in regard to

EXHIBIT 4-2: SECOND-GRADE CLASSROOM

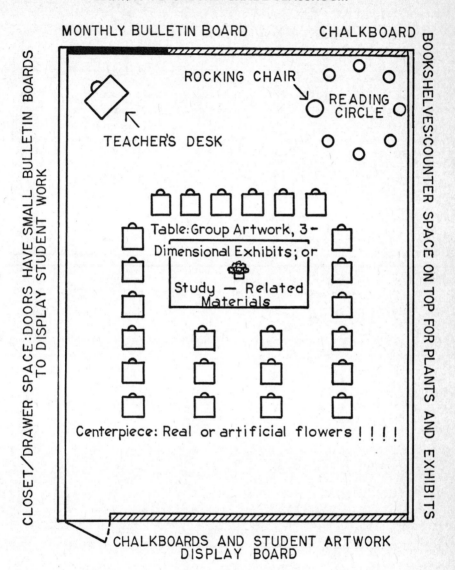

their teacher, themselves, and their studies. Not surprisingly, it was a great year for both teacher and students!

EXHIBIT 4-3: DESK ARRANGEMENTS

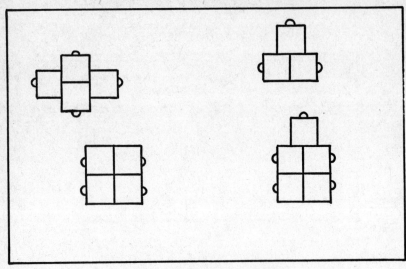

ISLANDS: DORIS TURNER

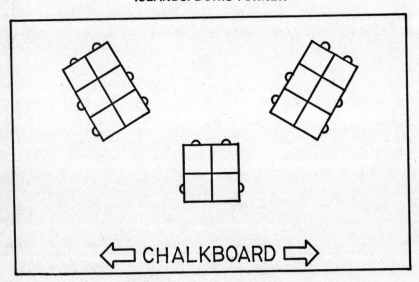

GROUPWORK COMBINATIONS: REBECCA GUESS

INCORPORATE DISPLAYS AND EXHIBITS WITH SPECIAL CHILD-APPEAL

Does it help to include interest-eliciting displays in your classroom? A majority of A+ Teachers think so! More than half of the ones surveyed *always* have student work displayed, and make extensive use of classroom exhibits in general.

Nora Mitcham's *"reading smorgasboard"* is a display which has been successful in "turning her students on" to reading because it includes everyday materials—bills, containers, tickets, labels, coupons, advertisements, and the like. Activity cards challenge her students to solve problems like these:

- What is a child's dose of this medicine?
- What does the electric company ask you to do before sealing your envelope?
- What TV programs are listed for Friday at eight o'clock in the evening?
- When does the cents-off coupon for cereal expire?[3]

Josephine J. Owen incorporates students' work in giant *wall displays*. These include mystery stories and poems, photographs taken by students, and original comic strip drawings. At least one sample of each special assignment is put up, and it remains on display all year.

Her students also make their own *study-related displays*. When they were reading *Ivanhoe,* for example, they constructed a castle complete with drawbridge, heraldry, weapons of medieval times, models of war machinery, and other items which helped to bring the story "to life." This inspired further activities such as baking a fennel cake, designing unique coats of arms, and arranging a miniature museum for the hallway showcase.

Alice Purdes highlights her annual study of coins with a *student display competition* based on individually chosen research topics. Genuine display cases are borrowed for the students, and recognition is given for outstanding results. Here is Ms. Purdes' own description of an especially commendable exhibit:

> Mellany was so intrigued with our reading unit on India that she chose this country for her coin research theme. A piece of black velvet material lines the bottom of her display case. Her Indian coins are in white 2x2's on gold background rectangles. A picture of the Taj Mahal is in the center bottom. Her numismatic information is in a separate frame beneath her display light. She has also added a snake charmer to bring out the Indian theme.

Finally, that old standby, the bulletin board, can be put to a wide variety of creative classroom uses. You may, for example, add "learning appeal" as well as "eye appeal" to your classroom by incorporating . . .

Student-centered bulletin boards. Mrs. Ray Winkler uses student photographs for attractive holiday displays, imposing faces on Christmas tree ornaments, Halloween figures, Easter eggs, and so on. My third-graders were delighted with our student silhouettes, which we displayed along with their autobiographical compositions. Classmates and visitors tried to guess who was who, and fun-filled questions challenged students to find out who likes to fish, who was born October 12th, who has hamsters, etc.

Theme bulletin boards. Mary Payson has had great success with a monthly art appreciation bulletin board honoring the "artist of the month." The exhibit includes a picture of the artist, biographical data, and copies of his or her masterpieces—along with related research and art work done by the students.

Three-dimensional bulletin boards. Gloryl Parchert has her elementary students project and trace large maps of countries being studied, right onto the paper-backed bulletin board. They are painted by the students, then made to "stand out" as much as possible. Cities are represented by tiny, colorful styrofoam balls, minerals by samples in pill bottles, agricultural products by "the real thing," and so on.

Mind-expanding bulletin board displays. Jean D'Arcy Maculaitis nails a pair of house shutters to the sides of a large bulletin board to transform it into a "window on the world." This serves as a backdrop for ever-changing displays of international news items and pictures, as well as student commentaries on current world events.

SET UP CENTERS THAT WILL MAKE LEARNING ALMOST IRRESISTIBLE

Top-rated teachers make significantly greater use of in-classroom learning centers. This is particularly true of elementary teachers and teachers with more than twenty years of experience.

What do centers contain?

A center may include just about anything: books, puzzles, experiments, models to be assembled or studied, free-expression materials, self-correcting activities, pictures, student-operated equipment, student projects, commercial materials, and the like.

A *Listening Center* in Estrela Lopez' classroom contains a tape recorder with several sets of ear phones and taped instructions on a wide variety of topics, with related worksheets and answer keys.

Eva Korth's *Math Center* includes a balance scale with weights and a variety of items to be used as counters, an abacus, meter sticks, a trundle wheel, a clinometer, a measuring tape, a stop watch, liquid and dry measures, an egg timer, a plumb bob, and both commercial and homemade games and manipulatives. These devices come to life thanks to Mrs. Korth's activity cards, problem cards, idea cards, and assignment cards (either purchased or made) which contain questions and activities to interest and challenge the students.

Judith Sorrenti makes her own cards for her *English Center* and encourages students and interested parents to also prepare some. These "fun cards" usually suggest enjoyable activities related to areas of study, and are illustrated with colorful drawings or magazine pictures. Exhibit 4-4 is one which was made for the study of similes.

How are centers used?

Harold Cotler describes his basic center as a table (or sometimes a wall or bulletin board) where students can read, write, choose idea cards, and select independent tasks for *supplemental work*. On a given day, two or three centers are in use, with students participating on a rotation schedule. Rules are made by students and teacher together regarding the use of their Creative Writing, Math, Social Studies, Science, Art, or other centers.

Charles Zeichner periodically uses what he calls "station math" with his junior high school students for *reinforcement* of recent learnings. Several centers with activity cards, calculators, overhead projectors, etc., are set up. This eagerly anticipated bi-monthly "treat" has helped tremendously in clarifying and reviewing important mathematical concepts.

Margaret Simpson's students use a variety of learning stations when required work is completed; Carol Hoffman issues tickets to her students designating which center to use that day; and Lois K. Smith notes specific center activities on student contracts. All three teachers stress that centers should be constantly changing with new ideas being added or new *themes developed*.

In Ms. Hoffman's class, the theme "We Smell with Our Noses" was developed through learning centers. One center featured experiences with scented clay, another related science experiments to the sense of smell, a reading center and a writing area were filled with

EXHIBIT 4-4: STUDENT TASK CARD

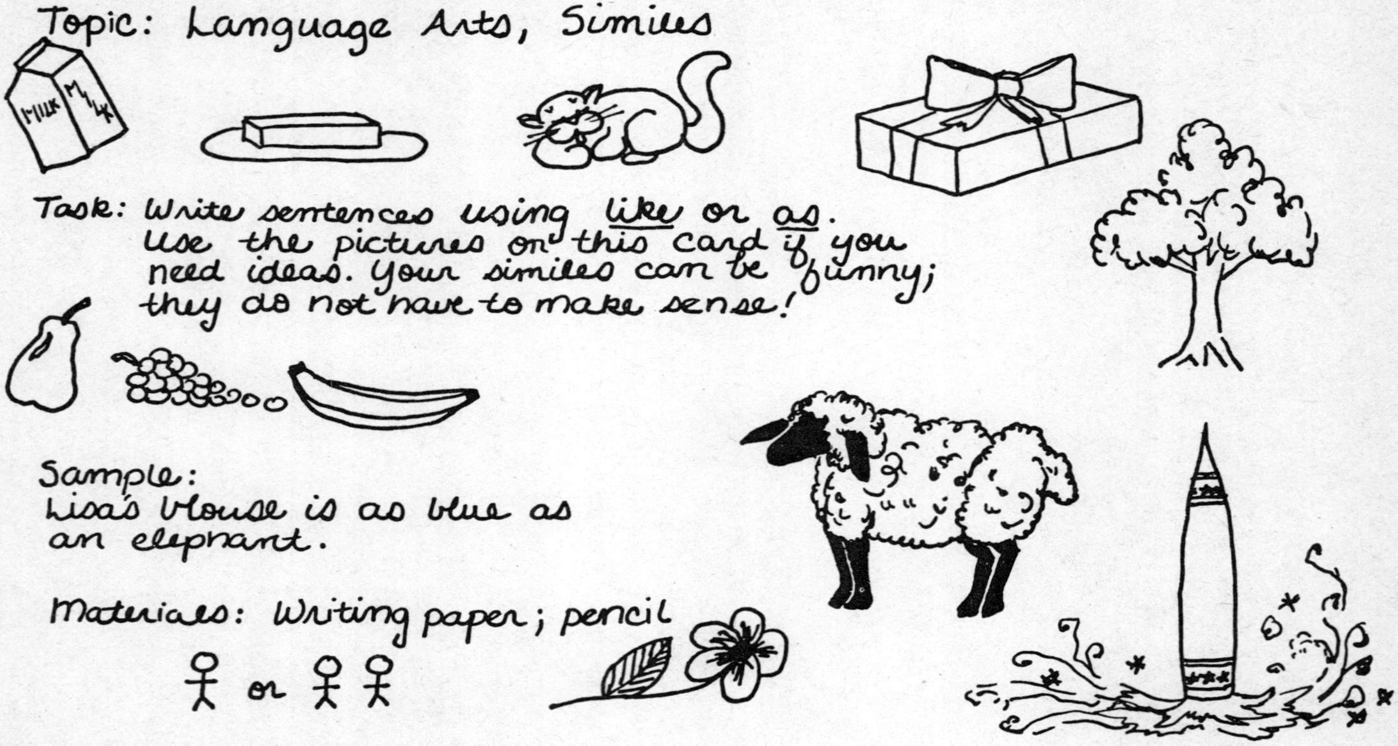

Topic: Language Arts, Similes

Task: Write sentences using like or as. Use the pictures on this card. If you need ideas. Your similes can be funny; they do not have to make sense!

Sample: Lisa's blouse is as blue as an elephant.

Materials: Writing paper; pencil

46

pertinent books, articles, and task cards, and a filmstrip projector was set up at another station with a special film and question sheet.[4]

CUSTOMIZE YOUR CLASSROOM—MAKE IT UNIQUELY YOURS!

Every room regardless of subject or grade level, can have something which distinguishes it from all other classrooms in the world. Taking your cue from A+ Teachers, you may, for example:

Create "special places" in your room

Doris Kneppel has a *media center* where students get to use audio-visual equipment; Gunnar Horn has a *cartoon display area* which keeps his students laughing; and Sharon A. Watson has a *self-service corner* where her kindergarteners get their own materials or supplies and clean up afterwards without adult supervision.

Eleanor Foley color-codes *special work areas.* The math area, for example, is blue, including all counters, shelves, tables, and trays for Math work. All Math materials are marked with a blue dot. This helps students and teacher to keep the room "organized," and it creates different "atmospheres" in one and the same classroom.

Lettie Siddens' *"contemplation corner"* is almost always in use. A large carton is turned on end (see Exhibit 4-1) as a hideaway where a student can get a few moments of relief from the hustle and bustle of the classroom. A nearby display, related to areas of study, offers some "food for thought." A grandfather clock was the center of this display when the class discussed nursery rhymes, a chicken coop during a study unit on farming, and a rocket model when outer space was being explored.

Put something out of the ordinary into your room

What is more unusual than a *bathtub* in the classroom? in Faye Shaw's classroom, it is a favorite "reading nook" for her students! Upper-graders may prefer *graffiti boards* for artistically expressing their individuality. One New Jersey teacher tried this with such success that his principal decided to have similar boards installed in the school's restrooms—which have been graffiti-free ever since.[5]

Sarah Schreiner finds a *full-length mirror* to be of great value in her classroom. Her kindergarteners enjoy trying on costumes, masks, hats, or glasses with built-in noses. Students learn about themselves and their friends by observing and by creating their own mirror games.

Using 2 x 4's, plywood, and carpet remnants, my third-graders built a *platform* that became the center of attraction in our classroom. It served as a reading or working area for individuals or small groups, and at the end of the day it became the stage for our daily "show." Sometimes a pantomime or playlet was presented, a story read, or a special lesson taught there.

A large *"teaching cart"* containing shelves, storage places, and a smooth Formica top was a noteworthy addition to Debbie Doherty's classroom. Also dubbed "The Roving World of the Metric System in Home Economics," it held metric charts, rulers, cooking tools, scales, and ingredients, enabling students to make an enjoyably delicious transition to the metric system. Once students mastered the metric system, they rolled the cart to other classrooms to share their knowledge through "metric mini-lessons."[6]

Do something original with the room itself

By doing something new or unexpected with your room, both you and your charges can receive a much-needed "lift" when spirits "sag." With a little imagination your classroom can become just about anything:

- *An airplane.* Students in Sophia Hoffman's class transformed their room into the interior of a modern jet. Chairs were arranged accordingly and flight attendants manned the aisles, serving refreshments to the travelers who "saw" the land to which they were going through dramatic presentations, research reports, a film, and a guest speaker.[7]

- *A TV station.* Foreign-born secondary students in Jean D'Arcy Maculaitis' classes made their room into a studio, where they wrote scripts, designed "sets," and video-taped newsreels about their native lands. For added authenticity they even had a recording of a teletypewriter as part of the sound track.

- *A whole new environment.* Junior high school students in Frank Schuenemann's Science classes often find that their room has—with student-made props and "decor" or through the mind's eye—been magically transformed into startlingly different surroundings: a living brain cell, a tropical rain forest teeming with life, Earth in the year 2001, or a galactic

battleship on the way to Jupiter. They perk up, their attention span at least doubles—and they apply their knowledge
to the tasks at hand with new-found vigor!

* * * * * *

When the classroom itself is something special, chances are
greatly increased that students will also view learning as
"somethin' special." When room arrangements vary
according to the ever-changing needs and desires of those
who work there (and when displays, exhibits, learning
centers, and perhaps even live animals add new and exciting
dimensions to studies), the stage is set for that kind of
enthusiastic and wholehearted student performance which
is worthy of a standing ovation!

* * * * * *

5 MULTIPLYING STUDENT LEARNING WITH INEXPENSIVE AIDS AND EQUIPMENT

What types of materials do superlative teachers use to give meaning to their subject matter and verve to their students? You may be surprised to learn that it is not the use of complicated and expensive aids that sets A+ Teachers apart from Others, but the more frequent and creative applications of everyday props. To illustrate, let's compare two fifth-grade teachers who are involving their students in the study of American Indians:

Teacher 1 does the following:

1. Has students read and discuss related textbook materials.
2. Duplicates material for information, worksheets, and student assignments.
3. Uses related commercial aids, films, and teacher-made materials.

Teacher 2 does the same, but also:

4. Uses the tape recorder for Indian poetry reading by the students, sharing of original short stories, and for recording the sound portion of a student-made film.
5. Uses the phonograph to present Indian music and well-known legends, and to introduce students to interpretive drama and dance.
6. Offers students opportunities to create Indian mosaics from scraps of colored paper, to make seed collages on styrofoam meat trays, to design colorful sand patterns in empty soda bottles, and to see what else they can do

with discarded or inexpensive materials.

7. Highlights the study with a student-made museum which displays basketry, weaving, leathercraft, beading, models, booklets, maps, paintings, and other student-made items. Parents and other classes are invited, and fifth-grade "tour guides" are armed with fascinating facts about the display pieces.

8. Purchases—with his or her own money if necessary—any materials deemed to be important.

Obviously, teacher #2 makes greater use of available materials and equipment, for more imaginative purposes.

This chapter sets before you a host of exciting ways in which A+ Teachers:

- **put the record-player back into commission,**
- **let the tape recorder "sound off,"**
- **give new "life" to throw-away items, and**
- **make optimum use of student-made teaching aids.**

See how many new (*and* old) ideas will come to mind as you read about how ordinary materials and equipment can be put to extraordinary educational uses. Think of ways in which you, too, can . . .

GET MORE "MILEAGE" OUT OF THAT OLD STAND-BY, THE RECORD PLAYER

The phonograph is a relatively inexpensive piece of equipment offering an endless variety of auditory experiences for students. It can provide accompaniment for fitness exercises or for games of "musical chairs," and when used with ear-phones it can open up a myriad of individualized and small-group learning activities.

Winnefred M. Haugland is always on the lookout for original ways to put her record player to good use—and she finds them!

- She has her third-graders walk the *mathematical number line* to music and write stories to go with certain musical works.

- She encourages children with perceptual awareness problems to *"act out" descriptive phrases* like "the big, heavy bear," "the scurrying squirrel," and "the hopping rabbit" after hearing them sung on the phonograph.

- She lets "problem students" *role-play feelings* to phonograph music. Take, for example, Harry, who had trouble expressing his feelings in a positive manner. When he took the part of an angry schoolmaster and let himself go to the mood of the music, his own anger changed to pleasure, excitement, success!

- She puts the record player into action to *promote talents and interests.* Cherie, who loved to dance, did some research about how children in other lands dance and borrowed records from the library. She learned a great deal and "blossomed" as she became a South American dancer . . . a Spanish señorita . . . a Bavarian "toe-slapper" . . .[1]

Records have been used in my own elementary classroom to *reinforce learning and encourage creativity* in the following ways:

- Learning *basic arithmetic facts* to a rhythmic beat or "catchy" melody.

- Writing endings for *story records* that are stopped at propitious places.

- Creating *songs about our studies,* to familiar musical accompaniment. For example, when we studied fire safety, we composed this special song to the tune of "The Man on the Flying Trapeze," one of the many orchestrations we had on a commercially prepared record:

    "Don't try to use fire
    Till you know what to do,
    So listen real closely and we will tell you:
    Be careful with matches
    And don't smoke in bed,
    And don't leave a fire till it's dead!"

- Improving *student penmanship* while developing an appreciation of many different types of music. Students listened to and discussed classical, folk, spiritual, jazz, country and western, Dixieland, rock, and other selections while working on their individual penmanship exercises.

Margaret Wolf, an elementary school Spanish teacher, uses

commercially prepared records to help children with their *Spanish pronunciation*, and Maralene Wesner has created her own records to accompany her own original *filmstrips*. Among those she has had published by Eye Gate are "Billy Ballad's Hootenanny" (a program of American folk music), "Lettie Letter" (beginning manuscript and cursive writing with jingles and cartoons), and "Exploring with Riddles and Rhymes" (a series of twelve reading units including original poetry by Mrs. Wesner).

MAKE STUDENTS "FEEL LIKE A MILLION" WITH A $30 RECORDER

An equally practical and no less exciting teaching device is the tape recorder—another piece of equipment used significantly more by outstanding teachers. As you consider the vast potential of this small machine, you will probably want to explore the great variety of educational tapes available commercially. Do not, however, overlook the unique and uplifting power of *"homemade tapes."* Your students will be delighted when you . . .

Draw them into active learning with your own tapes

First-graders in Maureen Buckmiller's class burst with pride as they work independently on *self-correcting activity tapes* prepared by their teacher. Appealing worksheets which accompany the tapes add to the joy of accomplishment experienced by her students.

There are no passive listeners to Ruth Townsend's *action tapes* either. These recordings elicit student participation, laughter, and excitement. For example, when listeners follow recorded material about apple farming from a resource book, they may find instructions like these sprinkled throughout:

- "Raise your hand if you like apples."
- "Show, with the correct number of fingers, how many trucks are filled with apples in the illustration."
- "Read this page out loud with me."
- "Now stand up and sit down five times before we go on to the next page."

This type of active involvement helps not only to hold student attention and to reinforce comprehension of the material, but it also allows Mrs. Townsend to see at a glance how carefully her students are listening!

Douglas Groff sparked student imagination and enthusiasm when he became a guide on a *touring tape* about the Golden Age of Athens. He took his "tourists" through the ancient city and described in detail the Acropolis, the Parthenon, the Market, and the homes of various Athenians. His students had never been called upon to "see" so much in their mind's eye, and they found the activity rewarding far beyond their expectations.[2]

Students in Don Gibson's individualized Mathematics programs are neither frustrated nor bored when they use his *teaching tapes*. These enable them to tackle new material when ready and to listen to explanations as often as necessary. These recorded lessons tie in with "plates" which contain examples and assignments. Exhibit 5-1 shows one of the plates which is explained on the taped lessons for Fractions.

Increase their exuberance two-fold by putting the "mike" in their hands

When Brenda Pena reads her elementary students a story, she usually records it for her *read-along library* so students can sharpen their reading skills by following along with the tapes. She has found, however, that they try doubly hard to read with fluency and expression when she gives them the opportunity to record their *own* selections.

Students in Mrs. Ray Winkler's class use the tape recorder themselves to share good poetry, to store important information on a subject in study, and to add authenticity to their own creative efforts. The same students also make their own *remedial tapes* with their teacher, organizing and preparing explanations and practice activities in their weaker areas. After they "test out" their own tapes, they put them into a special classroom resource center for others to use.

The recorder can be equally helpful in *pre-recording performances* or narrations for puppet shows. Once the words are on tape, the students can concentrate on the other parts of their presentation. This eliminates tears, embarrassment, or loss of dignity due to "stage fright," and it prevents the program's message from being clouded by unclear or forgotten lines.

EXHIBIT 5-1: TAPE RECORDER PLATE

PLATE 1A

CHANGING FRACTIONS

EXAMPLE 1:

$$\frac{4}{6} \qquad \frac{4 \div 2}{6 \div 2} = \frac{2}{3}$$

EXAMPLE 2:

$$\frac{10 \div 5}{25 \div 5} = \frac{2}{5}$$

RULE: $\dfrac{AC}{BC} = \dfrac{AC \div C}{BC \div C} = \dfrac{A}{B}$

CHECK YOURSELF!

DO WORKSHEET 1A

**RECYCLE SCRAPS RATHER THAN
"SCRAPPING" THEM**

The price of educational materials is not necessarily in direct relationship with their educational value. What is improvised or "created from scratch" may well be better geared to classroom needs than the more elaborate and expensive items. Elementary teachers are particularly good users of scraps and left-overs—and publications like "Pack-o-Fun" are excellent sources of ideas for creative utilization of the most unlikely materials. [3]

One A+ Teacher admits to having 1,000 paper cup lids, a large sack of pine cones, a tall stack of empty margarine containers, countless cores from plastic wraps, upholstery scraps galore, and a length of telephone cable in her classroom. She uses these for specific activities or as part of an "aesthetic arts center" in her room where students explore, discover, and create for themselves.

The following are specific examples of how items generally without value can be part of exciting and enjoyable learning experiences:

- *Environmental collage!* Students pick up and bag things on a walk in the school area. Emptied onto students' desks, the contents are arranged on 9x12-inch paper. Discussions relating to Science, Social Studies, Language Arts, etc. invariably ensue.

  Rebecca Guess

- *Grab bag surprise!* A wide variety of scraps and odds 'n' ends are concealed in a box or bag to elicit oral responses and guesses from students. Items are finally taken out, and students organize them according to usefulness, size, the five senses, color, or whatever other criteria they may apply.

  Hazel Morton

- *Recycled media!* Potato chip cans covered with colorful paper serve as containers for word game cards; foam packaging materials turn into manipulatives for number-matching games and regrouping activities; covered pie tins convert to word wheels and number games; discarded fish bowls set the stage for "fishing" games (for number problems, research topics, spelling words, etc.); and maps or workbook pages become re-usable activity sheets when covered with clear "Con-Tact" paper.

  Mary C. Holden

- *Catalog capers!* Old catalogs make attractive resource books. Students can search for words with certain vowels or letter sounds; they can practice Math skills by "purchasing" several items; they can find a picture to inspire creative writing; or they can create guessing games like "The Price Is Right."

Brenda Pena

- *Panelling pals!* Squares, triangles, rectangles, and other shapes are made from scrap pieces of panelling and used as learning aids. They are helpful in teaching identification, classification, measuring, determination of diameters and areas, etc.

Edwin R. Mitchell

- *Textbook resurrection!* Discarded textbooks are transformed into "new" books for individualized instruction. Stories from old readers are covered with student-made "story jackets." Activities from subject books are categorized and put into acetate folders for student use.

Eva Korth

- *Retain-a-container!* Partitioned liquor cases become student mail boxes and facilitate the distribution of papers and notices (Wanda Ward); packing boxes serve as learning center tables and can later store the contents when the center is disassembled (Diane Mazzei); and empty food or cereal boxes spark activities in all subject areas—calculating price per unit weight, studying food and mineral content, researching related occupations, preparing advertising campaigns, and so on.[4] (James M. Muller, Jr.)

Discarded materials can also be used for fun activities, handicraft ideas, and artistic endeavors. Consider these:

- *Glorious gifts!* Plastic spray container tops make mini hanging baskets in which enthusiastic students plant flower seeds. For larger hanging baskets, scraps of remnant fabrics convert clay flower pots to attractive planters, suspended from scraps of twine.

Doris Turner

- *Junk sculpture!* Salt boxes and other cylindrical boxes make excellent animal torsos. Towel rolls covered with plaster of Paris become legs and neck. Painting adds the final touch! Most anything can become a puppet—fly swatter, potato brush, flexible tubing. For truly original art forms, tape anything together, cover with plaster of Paris, and paint.

Alice Kihn

- *Toy for play, basket for May!* For fun and motor skills development, scoops are fashioned from large, plastic bleach bottles (see Exhibit 5-2). Two scoops, a ball, and two children make a good combination! A lovely May or Easter basket is created from the bottom of a bleach container, with a handle cut from the remaining part (see Exhibit 5-3).

Sarah Schreiner

EXHIBIT 5-2: SCOOP

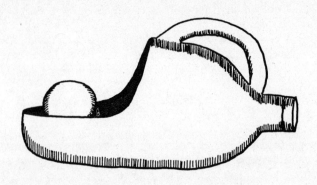

EXHIBIT 5-3: MAY BASKET

DOUBLE LEARNING POWER WITH STUDENT-MADE TEACHING AIDS

A significant difference between a "so-so" teacher and a "super" teacher is his or her ability to interest students in making, and using, their own teaching aids. Inner-city teachers are, according to our survey, especially adept at doing this.

Doris Turner's sixth-graders made *"parts-of-speech flowers"* when they studied different types of words. These construction-paper flowers then decorated the classroom as helpful reminders. Exhibit 5-4 shows three samples.

EXHIBIT 5-4: PARTS-OF-SPEECH FLOWERS

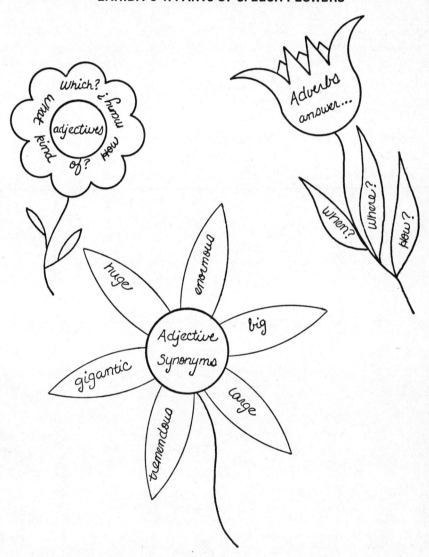

Lettie Siddens' primary students *make* and *use* a wide variety of their own learning aids. Among their favorites are *"Dial-a-Word"*

and *"Dial-a-Fact" telephones* like the one in Exhibit 5-5. The two parts, cut from posterboard, are joined together with a paper fastener, and the dial is moved to change the problems. Answers are listed on the back.

EXHIBIT 5-5: DIAL-A-FACT TELEPHONE

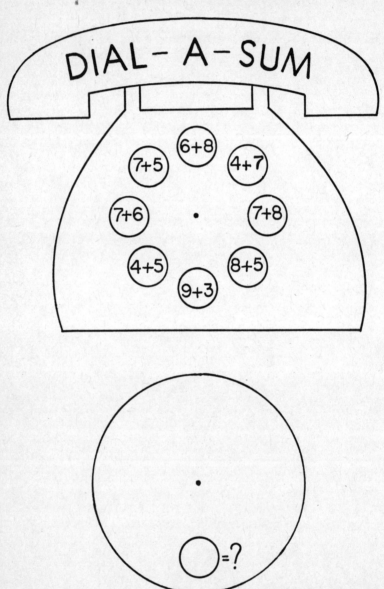

Janet L. Ryan's students work together to make *"letter lolli-pops"* consisting of paper discs stapled to tongue depressors. A letter is put on both sides—generally the same letter, one in lower and the other in upper case. Lollipops are used for memory and matching games, study and drill work with a partner, and activities like "buying" lollipops by recognizing and "sounding" the letter.

Rebecca Guess and her second-graders devise *reading wheels* for two-syllable or compound words (Exhibit 5-6), *"flip charts"* to study beginning sounds (Exhibit 5-7), and *"storybook helpers"* for vocabulary assistance (Exhibit 5-8). Such aids double, triple, and even quadruple classroom learning. They not only stimulate the students' own desire to learn, but they also motivate their friends and family to "come into the act" and to provide additional re-inforcement.

Alex Dobrowolski involves small groups of his junior high school students in creating their own *educational comic books*. Students analyze characterization, space layout, coloring, plot lines, printing, and advertising in commercial comic books before de-signing their own. Their finished products, based on historical events in their Social Studies curriculum, are passed from group to group for student study and evaluation. Soon the entire class consists of "experts" on comic book production—and American History! Exhibit 5-9 is the cover of a student-made comic dealing with the causes of the Revolutionary War.

"Learn from Each Other" activities are additional ways to "recycle" student work for the benefit of the entire class.[5] Task cards with assignments such as these get students to learn from, and elaborate upon, classmates' accomplishments:

- Study Nan's project on metamorphosis. Make your own illustrations.
- Read the story that Billy wrote called "The Happy Day." Make a listing of all the happy events it describes. Add several of your own to your listing.
- Scrutinize Dora's sculpture. Write a commentary, critique, fictitious news articles, *or* a letter of congratulations.
- Use Richard's electric answer board, noting your score. Try again. Make a bar graph comparing your two scores. Now either devise a new set of questions and answers for his board or design a new circuit plan for one of your own.

EXHIBIT 5-6: READING WHEELS

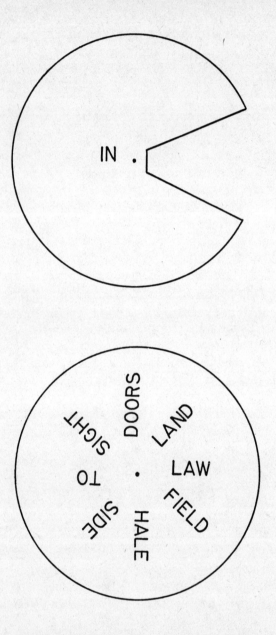

**CONNECT WHEELS WITH A PAPER FASTENER
AND TURN TO BUILD DIFFERENT WORDS.**

EXHIBIT 5-7: FLIP-CHART (FOR BEGINNING SOUNDS)

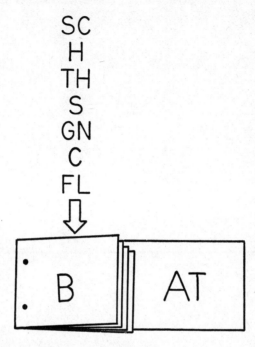

EXHIBIT 5-8: INDIVIDUALIZED VOCABULARY AID

BUY
TABLE
WHICH
STORE
NEED
LEFT
BOX
MONEY
EAT
CHAIR

LIST OF WORDS CAN BE PULLED UP OR DOWN THROUGH SLOTS IN MOUTH.

EXHIBIT 5-9: COMIC BOOK COVER

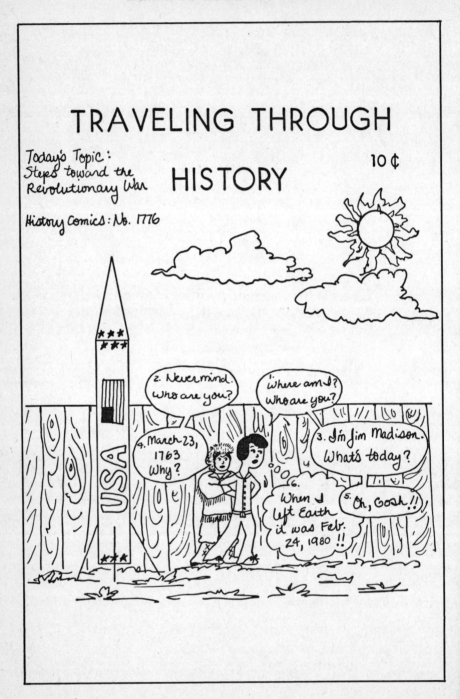

*   *   *   *   *   *

Does good teaching depend upon intricate aids and innovative educational hardware? Not at all! It expresses itself more aptly through the thoughtful and inventive employment of readily available, selectively purchased, and possibly even "found" materials.

These include the everyday record player, the simple cassette tape recorder, throw-away items, and original student-made contributions. It is the uncommon use of these very common materials which can multiply student learning and initiative in *your* classroom!

*   *   *   *   *   *

⑥ PREPARING THE PROPER EDUCATIONAL "DIET" FOR EACH OF YOUR STUDENTS

To what extent can, and should, the teacher adapt the curriculum to the individual student? To see what a difference individual accommodations *can* make in student attitude as well as aptitude, let's consider what one student, Alice, has gained from her teacher's flexible approach. Here she is now, speaking with a friend:

Joan: Hi, Alice! You sure look like the cat that swallowed the canary. What's the good news?

Alice: There's no special news. I'm just in a good mood because I'm coming from the best class of the day, Algebra.

Joan: Algebra? Ugh! It sounds awful!

Alice: If you had *my* teacher you'd feel differently.

Joan: I doubt it. Math of any kind has always been my weak spot.

Alice: Mine, too. But with Miss Davis I'm not doing so badly this year, and I really enjoy the class.

Joan: Tell me more.

Alice: Well, in Miss Davis' class I really feel special because I get lots of chances to "do my own thing."

Joan: Such as?

Alice: Action time! After we learn something new we get right to work, discussing and practicing what we've just learned. Sometimes I sit with friends and we give each other problems; sometimes Miss Davis summons me to a private "chat"; and at other times I work alone on all kinds of fun things. I especially like our "do-it-yourself deposit slips." These are papers with problems, and according to the number I get right, I can make a deposit in an imaginary savings account to purchase a "dream." I'm saving for my own swimming pool!

Joan: I need more convincing.

Alice: OK, in Miss Davis' class I don't have to worry about falling behind—or being held back, either. If I need help in something, I just have to write HELP on the chalkboard during action time and a "rescue squad" soon arrives.

Joan: What's a rescue squad? That sounds neat.

Alice: The first three kids to respond make up the squad. These are kids who are sure they know all about what we're studying and want to help.

Joan: I'm still listening.

Alice: And if I think I know enough to move ahead on my own, I can go to the "super selections box." I find lots of challenges there!

Joan: You know, it's hard to believe that Math can be fun. Don't you ever get tired of all those formulas and all that figuring?

Alice: We never get bored, if that's what you mean. You know Mark? Well, he wants to be an accountant some day; so he gets special accounting-type problems. Ted is always building things; so the teacher often asks him to show us how he uses Math in his construction projects. And Karen—she's "gung ho" for interior decorating. Do you know that Math can help her too?

Joan: And *you?* Has it helped *you?*

Alice: For me it's just lots of fun thinking up story problems about things I enjoy, like the one I did last night at home. It goes like this:

> "Alice swims like a fish. She is able to swim 60% faster than her older sister. So, when Alice swims 80 feet, how far has her sister traveled?"

Joan: Can you really swim so much faster than your sister?

Alice: Not yet, but if I can do so well in Math, then I surely can be a great swimmer some day if I put my mind to it!

Miss Davis is one of those Teachers who are more concerned with the teaching of persons than subjects. Not surprisingly, she is able to raise her students' self-esteem as well as the level of their academic accomplishments.

In the following pages, A+ Teachers from all areas of our country will present you with a variety of possibilities for:

- giving extra encouragement to slow learners,
- opening up new vistas for above-average students,
- meeting individual differences in student abilities, and
- focusing on the personal development of each student.

GIVING SLOW LEARNERS A "LIFT"

A+ Teachers, especially those with at least twenty years of teaching experience, are most likely to provide slow learners with extra aid and encouragement. Much of this additional assistance is given during the formative, elementary years, but a study done by the Stanford Research Institute found that older students gain even more from remedial work than the younger ones.[1] The following ideas, therefore, include suggestions for upper-grade as well as elementary teachers.

Organize some school-wide strategies

In River Vale, New Jersey, middle school students have access to a *teacher availability system.* Teachers who do not have a full schedule help students at designated times throughout the day. Thus, anyone who wishes to discuss an academic problem, needs one-to-one assistance, or has pressing questions about schoolwork will find a teacher ready to respond to that need.

Lola Lehman is the Learning Center Director at her elementary school, and a large part of her time is spent giving *small-group and individual assistance* to slower students. She uses individualized lessons for Reading and Math on a wide range of ability levels—planned in cooperation with the classroom teachers.

In an Arizona high school, Jane Brake volunteered to teach a special English course geared to slower learners. Seniors having problems and not planning to go to college take her *re-structured course,* which stresses practical uses of English and seeks to meet the unique needs of the group and the individuals within it.

Sheryl Hinman's junior high school in Illinois had another idea. The entire English staff took slightly larger classes so one teacher would always be free to run the "English Center." Here *remedial skill packets,* prepared commercially, by teachers, or by the students themselves, introduce and reinforce important skills for students who would benefit from this extra help.

Devise some in-class approaches of your own

Billy J. Pack schedules frequent *conferences* with individual students, during which he devotes extra time and attention to those who are falling behind. Miriam Moskowitz finds that *dividing study material* into smaller parts provides her slower students with the small successes that set the stage for "big strides" forward. She puts more complicated work into levels or steps, encourages students to seek assistance if necessary, and enables them to test themselves before proceeding to the next step.

Don Gibson prepares *special programs* for students who are weak in any of the areas covered by his individualized Mathematics program. For each of the twelve required study units, he has created simplified approaches (in terms of wordings used, amount of work assigned, and difficulty of practice problems). These are available to those students who need them. Few need the simplified approach for all units, but many need it in at least one or two areas.

Rinna Wolfe has an "each-one-teach-one" policy of *peer assistance* in her elementary classroom. In her system, students are always ready to explain, demonstrate, and share their understanding of the school work. Because it is not a formal program, there is no stigma attached and no lowering of self-esteem—just a friendly exchange between classmates.

RELEASING THE BRAKES THAT HOLD BACK THE GIFTED

The "super bright" or gifted students in America total at least 2,000,000.[2] There are millions more who are far enough above the norm to be in need of some extra educational "stimulation," and in order to meet the unique needs of these students, you may find that you have to:

Expand your curriculum

The most competent teachers, especially at elementary levels, are adept at identifying and helping the gifted students right in their own classrooms by adding depth and breadth to their educational programs.

- They may provide *individualized enrichment packets* consisting of a variety of student-selected worksheets which form customized booklets of challenging activities.

- They may set up *creative learning centers* with task cards, books, exhibits, special materials—and directions for their use in line with gifted students' unique needs.

- They may plan all-class activities encouraging *open-ended thinking* which serve the gifted without excluding others. Eva Korth, for example, has her elementary students concentrate on everyday items (like plastic cups, clothes pins, paper clips) to find new and varied uses for them. Rinna

Wolfe has her students search for alternatives for certain words. In one instance, a class came up with 187 replacements for "went."

- They may assign *sophisticated responsibilities* to gifted students to create "niches" for them in which they can sharpen their exceptional abilities and at the same time remain part of the class. Donald DeVries has a "lab foreman" help to plan and set up experiments for his junior high school Science classes; Cy Sommer uses a "production foreman" to assist in his high school Baking sessions; and other A+ Teachers use positions like "teacher assistants" or "assistant instructors" to open up new avenues for their gifted.

Go beyond the curriculum

Many times, the gifted may have to be excused from general classwork to be challenged with far more advanced or special assignments. Mario Fierros has prepared a *"super program"* in which outstanding high school Spanish students work independently, at the pace they desire, and on materials or projects of special interest to them. This relieves boredom and motivates the "linguists" in his classes to find their own levels of achievement.

Connie Anderson *pre-tests* in Spelling to spot students who are completely "out of step" with the others. When warranted, she exempts them from certain series of lessons and has them go on to much more advanced studies.

Williard C. Widerberg, a National Teacher of the Year, sometimes *"moves" students* who show exceptional ability. This may mean having the student proceed to another area within the course framework or into a more advanced class studying the same topic. If this is not enough he may even "promote" him or her into a higher grade for that subject!

Some *organized efforts* have also been made in recent years to support and encourage the gifted students. For example:

- In Englewood Cliffs, New Jersey, *independent study programs* are set up for the upper five percent of the students from kindergarten through grade eight. These students are excused from regular classes twice a week to enable them to work on special interest projects in classes of up to five students.[3]
- In California, *equivalency diplomas* can be earned by gifted students, enabling them to graduate two years early.[4] Other

school systems offer highly competent students *college credits* for courses taught by high school personnel under the supervision of college professors.[5]

- *Special programs,* local and statewide, are sometimes aimed at the gifted. A state-supported one in California provides at least three hours a week of advanced or specialized activities for the top 2% of the students and 1% of culturally deprived students with high potential.[6]

- *Enrichment workshops* like those run by privately operated societies, on Saturdays or during the summer, have much to offer gifted students. One "College for Kids" program, for example, gives capable students from 4½ to 16 years of age an opportunity to use college facilities for study of Marine Biology, Basic Electronics, Archeology, foreign languages, etc.[7]

WORKING WONDERS WITH A HETEROGENEOUS CLASS—IT CAN BE DONE!

Teachers sometimes become so concerned with "special" students at either end of the spectrum that they may overlook the uniqueness of the more average students. According to our survey, this is less likely to be true of A+ Teachers because they put significantly more stress on *individual* growth and achievement in their classes. Here, then, are some ideas for effectively coping with different academic levels so *no one* is neglected.

Rinna Wolfe schedules a weekly *research hour* for her fifth-graders. The librarian works with her to prepare a moving cart of books and reference materials on a wide variety of topics at different reading levels—so *everyone* can find meaningful pursuits.

My third-graders and I prepared our own *"activity encyclopedia,"* an ever-growing collection of learning opportunities encompassing all subjects and abilities. Each student retained his or her own copy as a handy reference for teacher-prescribed assignments, student-teacher planning sessions, homework possibilities, and free-choice endeavors.

Lily DeCleir originated a very successful *individualized reading program* to supplement the more formal instruction she provides in this all-important subject. Her students choose books from the classroom library to read for enjoyment, answer specific questions about the book, and discuss them with the teacher. Further individualization takes place as students share books with each other through story-telling, drawings, dioramas, skits, puppet shows, and other student-selected means.

A primary school teacher in New Jersey found herself unable to keep the class together in English because of the wide spread of abilities—and decided on *individualized English.* She categorized more than 100 skills and developed each with a series of acetate covered 5 x 8-inch index cards (like the one shown in Exhibit 6-1). These contain a rule or explanation, an example, some practice work to write onto a separate paper, and a chance for the student to creatively apply what has been learned.

The program also included workbook pages, independent record-keeping, self- and peer-testing with coordinated evaluation cards, frequent teacher-student conferences, and a wide selection of related activities for each topic. How did this new technique work out for this teacher? Her classroom became a "beehive" of active, individualized learning—and one substitute teacher almost "passed out" from the shock of seeing enthusiastic students get down to work even before the formal school day began!

Wally Bain created a *unique approach* to a high school Science course he teaches. In his program students individually complete sequenced "modules," or units of study, consisting of academic objectives, pre-tests, contracts, information and assignment sheets,

EXHIBIT 6-1: WORD STUDY CARD

B14 •
a

SAW stands alone. SEEN needs a helper (has, had, have).

Billy [saw] the show. Have you [seen] it?

Fill in saw or seen.

1. I [ ]____today.
2. The teacher [ ] that I needed help.
3. Had the cat [ ] the dog?
4. We have never [ ] it snow here in July.
5. _____

(Write your own sentence).

and post-tests. There is extensive use of audio tapes, slides, film-strips and film loops, books, laboratory equipment, and student ideas. Exhibit 6-2 shows the steps a student takes as he or she proceeds through each module. Optional activities involve students in designing original work to supplement the program.

EXHIBIT 6-2: SEQUENCE FOR INDIVIDUALIZED SCIENCE PROGRAM

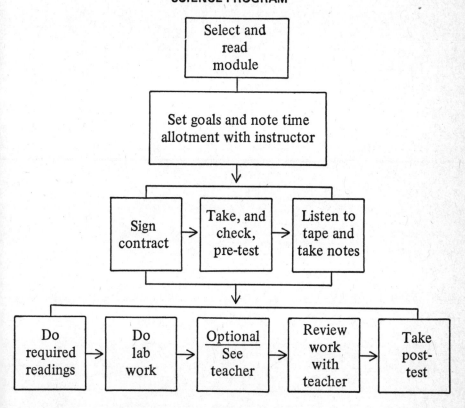

CATERING TO THE UNIQUE TALENTS AND INTERESTS OF INDIVIDUAL STUDENTS

A middle school student with a special talent in ventriloquism is encouraged to plan a program for an elementary class . . . a high school student paints a mural to brighten up the colorless hallways . . . an elementary student selects an aspect of Mexico to research during the class's study of that country.

A+ Teachers, especially those with many years of experience, have found that activities like the above are extremely effective because they capitalize upon students' individual preferences and abilities.

How to ascertain individual talents and interests

Conscientious teachers have developed a variety of methods to discover their students' special talents and interests. Milli Greene designed a *"wheel of concern"* for locating interests of church school youngsters, but her idea can also be helpful to public school teachers. Exhibit 6-3 shows an adaptation of this for the study of a country in Social Studies. Students color each section either fully or partially—depending on their degree of interest in the particular subjects.

EXHIBIT 6-3: INTEREST WHEEL

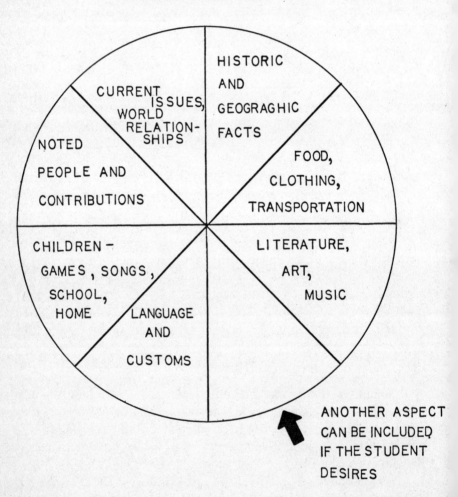

Eva Korth gets to the heart of student interests by using *interest inventory worksheets*. These contain incomplete sentences to be finished by her elementary students. Exhibit 6-4 shows one which she devised for Reading.

EXHIBIT 6-4: READING INTEREST INVENTORY

1. I like to read about . . .
2. In my free time I like to . . .
3. I like people who . . .
4. My favorite author is . . .
5. When I grow up I want to be . . .
6. I don't like books that . . .
7. I'd like to go . . .
8. My favorite time to read is . . .
9. The thing I like to read most is . . .
10. I like to read aloud to . . .
11. What I want most in the world is . . .
12. I like books with . . .
13. I wish . . .
14. Reading makes me . . .

Carl R. Berg continuously monitors his fourth-graders by asking them to fill in a *questionnaire* at the close of each school week. Students provide pertinent feedback with answers to questions like these:

- What school activity did you enjoy most this week?
- What would you have liked to do that was not done this week?
- What did you do outside of class that you would like to share with us?

How to tailor your approaches to these talents
and interests

Once the students' talents and interests are known, activities, projects, and assignments can be planned with them in mind. Some ideas that A+ Teachers have found to be successful include the following:

- *Voluntary field trips* for interested students to attend state legislature meetings, local council gatherings, and civic affairs in coordination with their studies (Mary Ann Brady).

- *Lunch hour discussions* for interested students to read and analyze great books. With guidelines and materials from the Great Books Foundation, teachers and volunteers involve students in reading selections from noted literary works and in discussing thought-provoking, interpretive, and opinion-type questions during lively follow-up sessions (Anne Chatfield).

- *Optional enrichment courses* offering junior high school students enticing subjects like Horticulture and Electronics during study halls, lunch hour, or the last hour of the day, which is an "interest activity period" for the entire school (Earl J. Montgomery).

- *Mini-group opportunities.* These are planned four times a year and consist of a week's study in many varied and fascinating areas. Students select their subjects and pursue them in small groups under the direction of their teacher (Willard C. Widerberg).

Teachers can help students to develop an interest in a subject by making it attractive or "special." I found that Reading suddenly became everyone's favorite subject when I prepared a *"Select-a-Story" program* from a variety of old reading textbooks. Lists of stories were devised, and each story was described with a "selling sentence" divulging just enough to arouse some healthy curiosity:

- Here's an exciting story for sports fans; don't miss the unexpected ending.
- Billy has a problem getting along with his sister. Read to find out how he solves it.
- Animals talk . . . fairies appear . . . and other wonderful things

happen! This is a delightful story you will want to tell your grandchildren some day.

Not only were children given a chance to read about subjects that interested them, but they were encouraged to take a renewed interest in reading, too. Their scores on specially-prepared question cards proved that as spirits soared so did reading abilities! Classroom resources also expanded as enthusiastic students prepared additional "selling sentences" and question cards for books and stories they had read and thought others might enjoy.

* * * * * *

A principal in Maine clocked the rate at which students responded to the fire drill bell. It took the kids *four minutes, thirteen seconds* to evacuate the building. Later the same day he clocked them when the recess bell rang. It took them *one minute, forty seconds* to clear the building this time.[8]

Ideally, students should race into, not out of school! This will only happen, though, when *all* students—the slow learners, the gifted, and the vast majority in between—receive the proper "diet" and find value, excitement, and personal meaning in the school experience.

And a good place to start is right in our own classrooms!!

* * * * * *

7 PROVEN METHODS FOR TEACHING—AND REACHING— YOUR STUDENTS

How do *you* teach? Do you stress drill, memorization, and other old-fashioned basics which have been neglected in recent years? Do you rely heavily on formal class lessons and full-group discussions? Do small groupings of students and individualized approaches abound in your classroom?

We will see what distinguishes A+ Teachers from the more average ones as we read a principal's letter of recommendation for a departing teacher—taking special note of the teaching techniques he describes.

To whom it may concern:

Joan Smith is a superlative History teacher who gave our school nine years of dedicated service. Her teaching methods have produced knowledgeable, enthusiastic, and grateful students. I have had the honor of sitting in on some of her class discussions and became so captivated that I simply could not leave. Her students were prepared for these discussions in a variety of ways: through special assignments, homework guidelines, small-group "pre-discussions," library visits, etc.—and the depth of understanding they exhibited was astounding!

Mrs. Smith is an advocate of small groupings, and never seems to run out of good ideas. She may, for example, "prime" several students to instruct a few classmates, line up student teams for a major project, or initiate peer drill sessions for memorizing and reviewing important historical data before a test.

She also gives special attention to the *individuals* in her classes, frequently working on one-to-one bases with them. She even created an individualized program to supplement her curriculum. The core of this program is an "a-la-carte-system" consisting of "fact folders" for those particularly interested in a topic, "fun quizzes" to check and reinforce knowledge, and "project suggestion cards" for creative and adventurous students. With these many opportunities available, every student finds challenging, rewarding, and often "personalized" enrichment experiences.

I consider Mrs. Smith to be one of those extraordinary educators who will always put forth a wholehearted effort . . . with amazing results! Our loss will most assuredly be your gain.

Sincerely,

William Briant, Principal

This letter is purely fictional, but the type of teacher it describes is factual. This is the person who, through hard work and a variety of teaching methods, brightens up the subject and lights up the lives of the students.

In this chapter, you will find award-winning ideas for:

- making drill-type work more appealing,
- bringing together the entire class with large-group discussions,
- initiating exciting small-group endeavors,
- reaching out to individuals within your class, and
- adding some "spice" by trying something different for a change!

Be on the lookout for little "sparks" of inspiration and insight for your own teaching as you contemplate how some of your most able colleagues:

TAKE THE BOREDOM OUT OF DRILL-LIKE ACTIVITIES!

Top-rated teachers neither deprive their students of drill work, nor overly burden them with it. According to our survey, Other Teachers are more likely to go to these extremes, whereas those known to be successful tend toward a "drill in moderation" approach, recognizing the vital need for this educational element, yet seeing the negative implications of too much rote-type learning.

Their solution, therefore, to the dilemma of whether to bore students with drill work or to eliminate it is to do neither! Instead, they make drill-type exercises less boring and more appealing. One way they do this is by *supplementing drill work* with activities that help the learners to understand, analyze, and creatively utilize the facts or skills being drilled. For instance:

- They may ask students memorizing basic Mathematics facts to *explain the processes* behind the facts, make their own progress charts, devise games and contests, "test" peers, or even challenge parents to solve problems and answer questions.

- Instead of requesting that spelling words be written five times each, they may invite students to a *word party* at which games are played, stories written, posters drawn, and lists of interesting "spin-offs" devised. Students will end up writing the words *several* times—as part of a fascinating and memorable "treat."

- When state capitals are being committed to memory, they may suggest some student *"detective work"* to find out more about these important cities. Newly-gained knowledge can then be put to practical use as booklets, flash cards, tour maps, travel guides, bulletin boards, and other "results" make it all worth while.

Research shows that students are more likely to succeed if tedious, drill-like tasks are made into games.[1] No doubt Donovan Holderness' Typing and Shorthand students attribute much of their success to their teacher's *"motivation books"* which contain hundreds of his "boredom breakers." These are enjoyable activities which give his students their much-needed practice while keeping interest levels high. Typing students, for example, may prepare their own cookbooks or learn to create their own "typing pictures" (like the one in Exhibit 7-1), and Shorthand students may reinforce their skills with a group competition like this:

EXHIBIT 7-1: ARTISTIC TYPING

TEN UP

Two sets of chalkboards are used. One person is sent to each board. The teacher says a word to be written in shorthand. If a student gets it right, a second student joins that team and another word is given. If this one is done correctly by both, a third player joins them. If a student misses a word, the entire team sits down and that team begins again. When ten students on a team get a word right, that group wins. (Students at their seats also write each word that is called.)

STIMULATE LEARNING AND FOSTER A "CLASS SPIRIT" WITH FULL-GROUP DISCUSSIONS

Lois K. Smith speaks proudly of the "esprit de corps" which permeates her elementary classroom; and Connie Anderson works hard to maintain the group cohesiveness which she has instilled in her students. Why? Because both outstanding teachers relate this intangible to the academic progress of their students.

When one well-known commercial program for individualized learning did not produce the dramatic gains expected, its failure was attributed to the exclusion of group instruction and discussion. "The group gives the activity importance," stated one evaluator. "The progress of the class is like a tide which carries all swimmers, though some are faster and some are slower." He went on to explain that without group interaction students will "hear individual notes," but may fail to detect the "melody."[2]

One good way to develop a productive type of "oneness," or group unity, is through the *large-group discussion,* an activity used significantly more by the highly acclaimed teachers.

In Don Gibson's individualized Mathematics program, students proceed at their own rates with tape recorded lessons, assignment sheets, special work papers, and a wide variety of independent choices. Important, too, are the periodic *"group days"* during which full-class lessons and discussions take place to clarify subject matter and make individuals feel a part of the "whole."

Maxel J. Ferguson believes so strongly in group discussions that he not only has them in English, but also in the *native languages* of his students, who to date have included Eskimo, Navajo, Chinese, Guamian, Appalachian, and Mexican children!

Mary Ann Brady uses the *"Socratic method"* of questioning during class discussions. In this approach her students are led, through carefully thought-out questions, to discover pertinent concepts for themselves. She makes these lively discussions, but is careful not to move them along *too* quickly because . . .

Patience in waiting for student responses can pay dividends, both academically and socially. In one experiment, teachers trained to wait at least three seconds before pressing for answers found that their students:

1. gave more detailed and thoughtful answers,

2. volunteered more often and showed increased confidence,

3. asked more questions and proposed more ideas of their own.

The teachers also noticed some differences in themselves as a result of the *longer "wait time."* Their opinions of students, especially the reticent or below average ones, changed for the better, as did their questioning ability and their responses to participating students.[3]

OPEN UP EXCITING POSSIBILITIES FOR THE SMALL GROUP

It is very likely that upon entering the classroom of an out-standing teacher you would find the students engrossed in some small-group enterprise. Elementary teachers, in particular, plan frequent small groupings to "fill a variety of bills": creating poems, learning to read, planning a party, completing an assignment, and so on. Such an approach can be extremely effective when it is used . . .

For more efficient learning

Homogeneous groupings often enable both teacher and students to use time more productively. Students with similar interests can be grouped for a project, students with similar needs gathered for a remedial lesson, and those with common abilities teamed up for rapid progress.

One California elementary teacher has found that *heterogeneous groupings* can be equally valuable. When students of varying interests and abilities share ideas and work together on small-group or com-mittee projects, they learn to agree, or at least to compromise. They also help each other out academically in this less formal atmosphere.

Chris Sabo gives her second-graders skill lessons in *select group-ings* of four or five students. She attempts to arrange the groups so that they contain at least one student who is proficient in the skill, one who is having difficulty, and others who fall "between." The lesson then involves a pooling of knowledge, a discussion of concepts and examples, and some actual practice of the skill.

To put student learning in the "active" rather than the "passive"

Small-group discussions elicit 100% participation from Mary Ann Brady's junior high school students who make careful preparation for discussing a controversial studies-related issue. A chairperson, a clerk, a "why" person, and an evaluator are chosen for each group to insure that:

- the group does not stray too far from the topic,
- relevant comments are recorded for a full-class follow-up,
- students remember to give reasons and supply information to back up their statements, and
- individual self-evaluations and a group rating are determined after the discussion.

Upper-graders in Jane Brake's English classes sit at tables, forming *autonomous groups* wherein each member takes an active part:

- A *table manager* conducts daily meetings with the group and oversees discipline at the table.
- A *payroll clerk* records bonus points which individuals at the table receive as they fulfill their academic responsibilities.
- A *bookkeeper* lists individual assignments and records extra-credit work.
- A *secretary* supplies paper and pencils when needed, and keeps track of books being read by each group member for book reports.
- A *file clerk* passes out and collects individual folders each day and is in charge of returned library books.

Ms. Brake enthusiastically reports that, both singly and collectively, students "blossom" and thrive in this set-up.

To add some "pizazz" to studies

For a special "twist," Ruth Allar sometimes plans *lessons culminating in small-group work.* When teaching introductory sentences, for example, she involved the entire class in a discussion of facts, ideas, and examples. Students were then put into small groups to select a topic and work together on the assignment. The following day the results were used as part of an exciting and enjoyable review.

Small-group competitions are highlights for the students in Miriam Moskowitz's Mathematics classes. She uses multi-step problems which give each student an opportunity to contribute to the final solution.

Students in Minnie Belle Churchill's Latin classes look forward to her *small-group practice sessions.* They may, for example, have "reading groups" much as they did in elementary school, to sharpen both their silent and oral reading skills with high-interest material. The only difference is that now they are reading in Latin, of course!

INDIVIDUALIZE WITHOUT "GOING BANANAS"

The most successful teachers, especially at elementary levels, spend more class time individualizing instruction than Other Teachers do. Brenda Pena, for example, prepares *activity folders* for the individuals in her class. Each student is given a large 10x13-inch envelope filled with enjoyable tasks gleaned from many sources, and thoughtfully selected with that particular child in mind. These exercises are completed during the child's free time or when required work is finished. A completed pouch is reviewed by the teacher, and then re-filled with new, often "made to order" challenges.[4]

Margaret Simpson of West Virginia finds a wide spread of abilities in her combination first- and second-grade classes; so she needs a variety of ways to "zero in" on individuals:

- For Penmanship she uses *worksheets* allowing students to work at their own levels and pace. Use of the chalkboard further glamorizes their handwriting activities.

- In Spelling, she pre-tests students and then forms three *homogeneous groups* for study and enrichment work.

- In Reading, those students who need extra practice read to her daily; those who are more independent readers branch out on their own in many directions.

- In Language Arts, she uses *learning stations* with individualized packets, worksheets, task cards, and lists of suggested activities.

- Each afternoon she has a half-hour *workshop period* during which students enjoy chess, drama, art, music, or just plain conversation. She also teaches macramé to interested students, and gets students to demonstrate their special interests and skills, too.

Upper-grade teachers are also finding ways to let students proceed at more individualized rates. Helen B. Guptill, for example, has prepared *Learning Activity Packets* (LAPs) to guide her junior high school Science students through the required material. These attractive, action-packed "learning packages" enable her students to move along at their own pace and give them ample opportunity to make choices, test theories, and discover many answers for themselves.

Edward E. Bowman has organized his English course for individuals by giving each student a *syllabus* of the year's academic work in the form of explanations, problems, activities, and student-chosen projects. As extra incentives, students get creative use of special classroom materials like a camera, a copy machine, and a small stage when they reach landmarks in their progress.[5]

INCLUDE SOME "SUPER SLANTS" TO PERK UP STUDENT INTEREST

Would your students vote "yea" for some added variety in *your* teaching methods? If you think they might, you may want to see which of the following ideas may help you to . . .

Bring it all together with themes and correlations

Lois K. Smith uses *saturation studies* in which she and her students learn as much as they can about every aspect of a subject or theme. Each topic, chosen for its relevancy, importance, and appeal, is under scrutiny for about a month—and all subjects are brought into play.

Upper-grade teachers can also work toward *combining subjects.* Margy Nurik and another teacher in her school work hard to overlap their respective Social Studies and English curricula. For example:

- The Language Arts teacher introduced *library research* with Social Studies material.
- Social Studies *vocabulary* was defined, alphabetized, and categorized in various ways as an English lesson.

- Proper paragraphing, punctuation, and other *writing skills* were taught in English class, then used in Social Studies for writing essays.

- *Newspaper reading skills* were introduced by the English teacher and reinforced by the Social Studies teacher as students designed their own historic newspapers.

- Students learned how to write *business letters* in English, then practiced what they had learned by requesting information, arranging for trips, and enlisting guest speakers for Social Studies.

Put it in contract form!

"Let's make a deal" is a proposition most kids cannot resist, and the contract is a good way to seal the agreement.

Students in Charles Zeichner's classes very willingly modify their disruptive behavior in response to his *discipline contracts.* Expectations are delineated and discussed, then both teacher and student sign and retain a copy of the document. For added motivation, students gain points, exchangeable for desirable rewards, as contract terms are fulfilled.

Carl R. Berg uses weekly *work contracts* with each of his students. The contracts list all the tasks to be undertaken during the forthcoming week: workbook pages, readings, Math assignments, *and* activities the child wishes to do when required work is successfully completed. Harold I. Cotler uses a similar approach with his students, using the contract in Exhibit 7-2 for planning and recording student activities.

Exhibits 7-3 and 7-4 show two more contract forms teachers have designed themselves. The first is a contract used by Shirley Moore on which students list goals, note their attainment, and record personal observations. The second is one prepared by Kent Schipper to help his students choose and organize a Science project.

Contract cards are among Jean D'Arcy Maculaitis' favorite teaching tools. These are 3 x 5-inch cards containing suggestions for independent and small-group projects, such as: "Plan a trip to Florida. Plot your route on a map, make motel reservations along the way, write up a budget . . . ." Students choose cards that appeal to them and sign up in a special contract book. Time allotments are noted, and students are encouraged to incorporate their own ideas and plan unique ways to present results to the class.

EXHIBIT 7-2: FIFTH-GRADE CONTRACT

Due Date ____________

I/We, the undersigned, do hereby resolve to do the following projects in relationship to the unit *New Jersey* in order to receive the award of *(a grade, free time, etc.)* upon completion of this contract.

> *(Here activities agreed upon are listed: readings, book reports, art projects, writing assignments, listening tapes, records, filmstrips, tests, etc. At least four activities are listed which include both basic and enrichment areas. Activities must be specific and clearly understood by all parties involved.)*

Signed, sealed, and delivered this *21st* day of *March*, one thousand nine hundred and ______.

Harold L. Cotler
(Teacher)

Jim Jones
(Student/s)

EXHIBIT 7-3: ELEMENTARY LEARNING CENTER
CONTRACT

CONTRACT

For _____

Week of _____

Job	Finished	Your Comments

_____
Teacher

_____
Student

EXHIBIT 7-4: JUNIOR HIGH SCHOOL SCIENCE PROJECT CONTRACT

PROJECT NAME _____

Briefly explain your project: _____

_____

1. List the materials you will need: _____
_____

2. Do you need to go to the library? _____
   How often? _____

3. Do you need to go off the school grounds?_____
   Where will you go?_____

4. When will you turn in your completed project?

_____

YOUR SIGNATURE:_____

TEACHER SIGNATURE:_____

SUGGESTED PROJECTS:

1. Collect 300 aluminum cans to keep the geological formations clean.

2. Clay, papier-maché, cardboard models of Round Rock, Tsaile Peak, Spider Rock, Fish Hook Point, Volcano, Syncline, Anticline.

3. Draw a map of the Canyon or other location in the reservation. This may be a drawing or a map enlargement using the opaque projector.

4. Stream table projects:
   a. Show effects of raising land.
   b. Show erosion of different land around Chinle.
   c. Design your own project.

EXHIBIT 7-4 (CONTINUED)

5. Reports on:
   a. Coal formations
   b. Oil formations
   c. Reservation soil
   d. Round Rock formation
   e. Mountain formation
   f. Continental Drift theory
   g. Lava bed formation
   h. Tsaile Peak formation
   i. Shiprock formation
   j. Spider Rock formation
   k. Sand Dunes formation
   l. Chinle Valley formation
   m. Flagstaff Mountains formation

6. Videotape your own project or one above. Include a demonstration or lesson with a written script.

7. Textbook projects: pages 284, 259, 244, and/or 245.

8. Speak to me about your own ideas.

Try "somethin' else"

Alice Kihn has very unusual helpers in her classroom—*teaching puppets.* These friendly characters, made from bottles, wire, plaster, and felt, actually teach the children lessons which include Handwriting, Reading, Speaking, and Listening. Particulary popular is "Spooky the Ghost," who assists students in sounding out Halloween words for creating really "spooky" stories.

Larry Schloer tries *musical approaches* with his students to help them memorize useful or important facts—and they love it! This well-known little tune, for example, was used to aid the students in recalling the linking verbs.

Am, is, are, was, were, be, been; now I know my linking verbs.

Harry H. Koch finds that *original Science experiments* are another good way to motivate student learning. He "revs" his students up by presenting challenging, thought-provoking activities like the sample in Exhibit 7-5. Students are given two or three days to think, do research, and work out their own solutions. Answers are then compared as the experiment is performed in class; but it doesn't end there. The completed experiment is left on display for a few additional days to stimulate further interest and discussion.

*   *   *   *   *   *

There can be no pre-determined method which works for all teachers in all circumstances. The only ingredient common to all success is the sincere effort of a caring, sensitive teacher who tries to teach and reach *all* students. Such an educator will naturally vary teaching approaches— not forgetting that effective drill-type work, dynamic group discussions, exciting small-group projects, and genuine attention to the individual student can make all the difference in the world.

*   *   *   *   *   *

EXHIBIT 7-5: SCIENCE EXPERIMENT

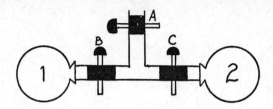

1. Open A, B, and C.

2. Close C.

3. Inflate balloon 1.

4. Close B; open C.

5. Inflate balloon 2 to half the size of balloon 1.

6. Close A.

7. When B is opened. . .

   a) will balloon 1 inflate balloon 2 until they are of equal size?

   b) will the two balloons remain the same?

   c) will 2 inflate 1?

8 DEVELOPING AN APPEALING ARRAY OF STUDENT ACTIVITIES

What types of day-to-day learning experiences do top-notch teachers plan for their students? Do their activities differ from those of other hard-working but less successful educators? Let's sit in on a student-teacher conference and watch for some clues.

Teacher: Did you enjoy our study of Switzerland, John?

John: Oh, yes, and I learned a lot. Now I won't mix up Switzerland and Sweden anymore.

Teacher: I see on your study evaluation sheet that you enjoyed the map-making activity and working on the model of the Alpine village, and you made a number of additional suggestions for class activities. Where did you get so many good ideas?

John: Well, last year when we lived in Washington I had a really great teacher; so I just put down some things we did in his class.

Teacher: You mention skits. Would you like to prepare one for the class?

John: Sure, but could I work with three or four other kids like we did last year?

Teacher: That's a good idea! But before you go to select your committee, let's take a quick look at the other ideas you listed. What kind of games did you have in mind?

John: Games like we had last year: big class contests or quiet, sit-down games like "Check the Checker."

Teacher: How did that work?

John: We had a big board with giant checkers. Each checker had a question on one side and the answer on the other. To jump that checker you had to know the answer. And if you didn't, the other guy would turn it over, read the answer, and then put it back on any space!

Teacher: That sounds like fun.

John: And my last year's teacher often had visitors come—and took us on trips, too. Hey! I know! Maybe my Uncle Bert could come and show us his slides of Switzerland.

Teacher: And what about a trip? Where should we go?

John: (hesitating, then beaming with sudden inspiration): To Switzerland, of course!

Obviously, John's *previous* teacher rates an A+ in activity planning. In addition to stressing practical, creative, and "hands-on" kinds of student activities (like the mapwork and model construction), he makes good use of classroom visitors, role-playing, student committee work, field trips, and games.

This chapter will show you how some of America's most effective teachers:

- add a special "attraction" to learning by bringing in guest speakers,
- get students "dramatically" involved,
- engage students in exciting small-group endeavors,
- extend learning beyond the school itself, and
- sprinkle studies with fun-type activities.

As you read about what other conscientious teachers are doing with obvious success, see how many ideas *you* can add which will . . .

MAKE YOUR CLASSROOM A "LEARNING MAGNET"

Part of having a dynamic class involves drawing others—*guest speakers,* classroom visitors, resource persons—into the flow of learning. The added information and fresh perspectives offered by "lay teachers" can both deepen and broaden the study topics—and perk up students in general! This is why A+ Teachers suggest that you and your students make a joint effort to open up your classroom to the electrifying power of knowledgeable and fascinating people.

Pull in study-related experts

This is just what Edwin R. Mitchell did for his sixth-grade Health units. He "cashed in" on the expertise of others. A variety of *experienced "pros"* from health-related fields helped out. The chairperson of the Health Department spoke on community health; a college Health professor demonstrated rescue breathing; a state trooper discussed the use and misuse of firearms; and the school nurse taught about the deleterious effects of drug abuse. The natural authority of these speakers increased the relevance of the topics and helped to convert what could have been a complacent class into a group of "magnetized" learners.

Guests hailing from Germany, England, South America, Pakistan, Kenya, India, and Japan imparted first-hand knowledge of their countries to the students in Lois K. Smith's and Lily DeCleir's classes. These *out-of-culture speakers* have been instrumental in expanding the geographical, social and cultural world of their students, while adding a depth and realism to their studies.

Enlist visitors who challenge students

If you find, as Connie Anderson has, that students need more experience weighing facts, recognizing opinions, and making independent judgments, try one of her "tricks": the use of *conflicting speakers*. Her students frequently hear two or more speakers present different sides of an issue. A bank executive, a stock broker, and a real estate salesman, for example, may talk about investing; and a conservationist, a zoo keeper, and a hunter might discuss their views of animal welfare. Students can then follow up with their *own* debates!

The use of *break-the-stereotype guests* is another way to foster student maturity. One such visitor in Moke C. Owens' Humanities classes will never be forgotten—especially by the boys, who found the particular skill taught to be much more rewarding (and difficult) than they had expected. Who challenged these students to change their thinking? A ballet instructor!

Try some special slants with special guests

If noted personalities are too busy to visit, they may be "game" for a *telephone conversation* with your class. One Pennsylvania teacher made arrangements to have telephone amplifying equipment installed in the classroom so students could talk with their congressman. The thorough preparation and follow-up efforts of the students, as well as the "chat" itself, made this an exciting learning experience! [1]

In River Vale, New Jersey, the junior high school teachers invited more than thirty people, representing a great variety of occupations, to visit for a *school-wide "Speakers Day."* Each student planned a schedule to attend a series of lectures in accordance with his or her interests, selecting from an enticing list of guests: doctors, dentists, secretaries, artists, actors, etc.

BURST THROUGH THOSE CONFINING WALLS

Just as attracting learning into the classroom is important, so stretching it beyond the four walls has powerful educational effects. *Outings*—large or small, far or near, highly organized or informal—need not be limited to the elementary and inner-city teachers who schedule them most frequently. Teachers at *all* levels and in *all* locations can use a variety of enjoyable and enriching field trip experiences.

Major excursions

Upper-grade students attending special courses at Donald R. Wilson's high school have *on-site learning experiences* using the Grand Canyon and other geologically interesting areas for "study weekends," and each year forty students in Wally Bain's Marine Science classes look forward to a week at a marine biology station. During this time they observe and work with marine biologists, putting to actual use all that they have learned.

Even elementary students are doing it! Connie Anderson's fourth-graders go on *weekend camping and hiking excursions* with her several times a year, and Rinna Wolfe's students planned a *five-day stay in Mexico,* taking on the responsibility of arranging for meals and transportation, making reservations for sight-seeing, and setting aside the necessary time to "digest" and discuss all they were learning during their stay.

Mini-trips

These are outings which are neither extensive nor expensive, but which can make a noticeable contribution to the students' education. Lois K. Smith calls hers *"hop-skip-and-jump" trips,* and these include just about anything within walking distance (such as a supermarket or a museum). Another teacher refers to these as *spur-of-the-moment "artistic walks,"* during which students make sketches, collect collage pieces, look for things to write about, or develop an appreciation for the aesthetic.

To Alex Dobrowolski, mini-trips mean nearby *jaunts with three-to-five students*—on his own time. These have included visits to local tombstones where brass rubbings were made, attendance at town events related to studies, and visits to landmarks of special interest.

Outings with a special "twist"

While studying community life, Margy Nurik's eighth-graders became *student guides* for a series of first-grade trips to the firehouse, the library, the municipal building, the post office, and the bakery. This turned out to be an astounding success for both the older and the younger students!

The same teacher also tried a *multiple field trip approach* during an elective course on Comparative Religion. Her students went on several field trips in nine weeks—in addition to having nine guest speakers visit. Residents of the community, faculty members, parents, and students not enrolled in the course were also invited to attend any, or all, of these special activities.

What you may not be able to do in actuality (such as taking that visit to Switzerland as John suggested), can sometimes be accomplished in an alternative manner (such as by viewing a travelog of Switzerland or by visiting an international airport to speak with Swissair personnel). Edward E. Bowman capitalized upon his students' desire to tour America by offering, instead, *"penpal trips."* Film was sent to other students across the country who took motion pictures of local scenes. The returned films were edited and narrated by the students and are now a part of the school library so other classes can "take the tour."

DELEGATE RESPONSIBILITY TO
STUDENT COMMITTEES

Small-group projects can work wonders according to Edith Widicus, whose class is composed of problem students aged 10 to 14. One such project involves the *creation of go-carts* from scrap lumber, wheels, and "found" materials. Three or four students work on each cart—designing it, building it, figuring how to make it work, and finally entering it in a class competition. The carts seldom last out the race, thus calling to the fore the students' "fix-it" abilities. Ms. Widicus considers this experience a real-life lesson in coordination, cooperation, and creativity—and it is one that is long and happily remembered.

The informality of the small-group setting can also be used to academic advantage, as Sister Mary Laubacher has found through her experience with *composition-correcting committees.* After discussing guidelines and examples as a class, her students break up into small groups to write their double-spaced compositions. These are then passed to all committee members for reading and initialed corrections. Each student considers the suggestions the others made and revises his or her paper, handing in both copies. Ever since these sessions have been instituted, the students have exhibited a greater awareness of what constitutes good writing—and they do a lot more of it![2]

LET DRAMA WORK WONDERS

Why do A+ Teachers—especially elementary teachers, inner-city teachers, and teachers with more than twenty years of experience—make greater use of drama and role-playing? They have no doubt found that activities like these are not only fun, but also educationally sound because they can be used in a multitude of ways for a great variety of teaching purposes. They can be used to:

Encourage creativity

An elementary teacher, Elizabeth Braden, prepares her own original *plays* which her students enjoy hearing, reading, and interpreting dramatically. Lita Grabeklis goes a step further and encourages her students to write and enact their own little playlets.

Small groups of students in Edwin R. Mitchell's class rewrite and *"modernize" fairy tales.* They then read and act out their stories to groups of younger children in the school, cleverly involving them in pinpointing and retelling the original versions!

One class of students overwhelmed their teacher, Ralph Caputo, with their ingenuity and creativity when they produced their own *mock TV show.* Their original production, "The Johnny Hartley Show," had a typical talk-show format: guests told of recent achievements, expressed opinions on important issues, displayed talents, discussed books, etc. For them, however, it was a 100% unique experience, right down to the "words from the sponsor" that they incorporated.

Improve basic skills

Barbara Webster uses *scripts of televised programs* to "turn students on" to reading. As they read and dramatize scenes they have seen (or soon will see) on TV, students sharpen both their reading and speaking skills.[3]

A *pantomime game* we called "Notes from Mother" helped my primary students to realize how necessary it is to know how to read, while "painlessly" improving their own reading abilities. We pretended that "Mother" had to go out unexpectedly and left a note on the table. After dramatizing the surprise of finding the house empty, the student would silently read, and follow, the written instructions ("Feed the cat, please"; "Will you set the table for me while I'm gone?"; "Don't forget to take the dog for his walk!"; etc.). Classmates then tried to guess the note's contents, which were finally revealed when the actor or actress read the message aloud.

Spanish teacher Margaret Wolf often has her students *dramatize everyday incidents* like two children meeting on the street, a child and parent going shopping, a teacher and student talking together, etc. The children wear hats, sarapes, and wigs and get to carry appropriate props. The only "hitch" in these little dramas is that all speech must be in Spanish. Ms. Wolf's stress on active and enjoyable student involvement, like this, is a main reason why her young students speak such good Spanish—and why they generally cheer as she enters the classroom.

Enrich studies

Donna Goldsmith found that her junior high school students enjoy preparing and presenting *content-related plays.* One student play about the Civil War included parts for slaves, plantation owners, reporters, President Lincoln, and so on. Through this activity, the study of abolition came to "life"—and afterwards students were anxious to plan similar activities for other study units. Social Studies took on new meaning as trials were staged, conventions re-enacted and other great events in American history protrayed.

Similarly, Wally Bain has his high school Science students create and present *dramatic interpretations of subject matter.* He offers students a choice of topics early in the school year, and they prepare their "dramas" knowing that the contents must be scientifically accurate, yet as creative as possible. One can well imagine the knowledge *and* imagination that went into productions such as "A Day in the Life of Harry Hemoglobin" or "Annie and the Pulsating Paramecia"!

Even *teachers* can have a part in the action. One teacher teams up with his principal to portray famous "duos" like Lewis and Clark, Edison and Ford, and Aldrin and Armstrong.[4] A Zoology professor at Berkeley University uses props and costumes to impersonate noted figures in Science (Beaumont, Harvey, Pasteur, Speman) who "visit" to lecture to his classes. He is not only making his subject more interesting but is evidently inspiring others in the art of role-playing—because when "Charles Darwin" made a scheduled appearance, an "ape" in attendance conscientiously took notes![5]

SATISFY YOUR STUDENTS' THIRST FOR FUN (AND YOURS TOO!)

Also characteristic of the best teachers (especially those with bachelor degrees or those who teach elementary school) is a greater stress on contests, games, and enjoyable educational activities. *All* teachers can appreciate the refreshing "lift" that activities like these can offer. Consider the following:

Class challenges

Students in Emily Ehm's eighth grade gain a special zest for their studies when they plan an all-out *challenge to another class*, another school, or even the entire faculty! One such activity was a student-initiated Spelling Bee between themselves and the school administrators. The youngsters put forth a supreme effort to prepare themselves for the big event, and during the match they even managed to teach the "experts" a thing or two about words like liaison and intramural. In the end, however, the administrators reigned victorious—but all participants had a marvelous time, and *all* acknowledged a greater competency in spelling.

Librarian Vivian Barnes sometimes challenges visiting classes to a *weekly "read-in."* Students enthusiastically choose and read their library books, then prepare a couple of paragraphs to read to her when they return the books. She sits in a chair facing away from the reader and attempts to name the book that is being read. Because she is familiar with most of the books in her elementary library, she usually wins out in this competition. The students are winners, too, though, because of their increased interest and proficiency in both silent and oral reading!

Group contests

Students in the junior high school classes of Charles Zeichner have fun gaining and clarifying subject knowledge when they play a game patterned after *"The College Quiz."* Mr. Zeichner has built up an ever-growing collection of question-and-answer cards for this major monthly event. Two teams of students compete, three per team, and after ten questions a new set of players takes over so all have a chance to play. To spark further excitement during the game, a surprise question is asked, and each team is able to wager any number of its earned points, double or nothing!

Barbara Payne uses another type of team approach with her Science students: *test review contests.* One way she does this is to have two teams vie for points by answering questions about their most recent study. Each individual within the team has his or her opportunity to answer, as question after question is given first to one team, then the other. "Stumpers" grow in value until they are either answered or put on a "better check it out" roster.

Enjoyable activities for all

A *carnival* to raise money for field trips, playground equipment, and extra classroom supplies is a yearly highlight for the students in Frank Estavillo's class. Booths are set up to sell ceramics, decoupage plaques, and a wide variety of other student-made craft items.

Also popular are *class-wide contests*—and "the sky is the limit" here for A+ teachers: essay contests, model airplane-making contests, rock identification contests, poetry contests . . . and the list goes on and on!

Don Gibson's Mathematics students enjoy the many types of *puzzles* and brain teasers he puts around the classroom for them to try in class or "sign out." Mrs. Ray Winkler makes up *action games* like "typewriter," a spelling game that her students frequently request. Each student selects a letter of the alphabet for the game, and as words are announced, the respective students jump up and call out their letters in proper sequence.

Finally, *quiet skill games* are a big "hit" with students because they mean individual, partner, or small-group enjoyment. Board games that Shirley Moore designs—with titles like "Batter Up" and "The Midget Car Races"—give her students memorable experiences with synonyms, rhyming words, telling time, etc. Another teacher, Miriam Moskowitz, shows her students how to make and use "Concentration" card games for learning and memorizing those all-important basic arithmetic facts.

* * * * * *

Do your students have to be constantly entertained at school? Of course not! A wise teacher knows, however, that an appealing array of student activities, including those which set top teachers apart from others (guest

speaker presentations, field trips, small-group endeavors, dramatic role-playing, and games), go a long way toward making student learning:

- come easier,
- stay longer, and
- have more meaning!

*   *   *   *   *   *

⑨ HOW TO PUT STUDENTS IN "HIGH GEAR" THROUGH ACTIVE INVOLVEMENT

When students spend too much time sitting and (appearing to be) listening—and the teacher spends too much time trying to get, and keep, everyone's attention—two things happen. Students get bored, *and* the teacher gets exhausted!

The "secret" to being an effective contemporary educator is putting your students' energy, and yours, to the greatest educational advantage. The teacher who wrote the following note to inquiring parents has apparently discovered how to accomplish just this!

Dear Mr. and Mrs. Williams,

Thank you for your interest in Brian's schoolwork. He is achieving and progressing well. He is an avid participant in our class meetings and is presently preparing a campaign for next month's presidency.

During our student-teacher conference last week, Brian expressed a desire to write his own "thesaurus" of antonyms to go along with our class study. It turned out beautifully, and he has already used it to prepare a special class activity for Valentine's Day. He made a page of two-piece "broken heart" puzzles, with a pair of antonymns in each. This was mimeographed and given to his classmates to cut out for a "mend the hearts" contest which he supervised.

Your son enjoys correcting his own classwork at times, and will often re-do a paper in which too many errors are found. He keeps his own checklist of accomplishments and is very capable in preparing and following schedules based on choices available to him. He recently gained the honor of "Master Speller" because he learned all fifty of his "most wanted" words. He also won the "Runner Up" award for the fastest mathematical figuring without paper and pencil!

As you know, Brian is very artistic—and his assistance in setting up our "Birthday Bonanza" bulletin board was much appreciated by all. We now have a lovely way to make everyone's birthday a special occasion. Please come in to see it.

Report cards will be sent home next month. If you have any further questions before or after, please write, call, or visit.

Yours truly,

Miss R. Stacey

Miss R. Stacey

Brian is not just sitting back watching his teacher tire herself out. He, too, is "on the go" because Miss Stacey works hard to get her students as actively involved as possible.

This chapter will present you with a variety of ways to:

- **give students responsible freedom in the classroom,**
- **develop student autonomy with class meetings and private conferences,**
- **keep students "on the move" with positive incentives, and**
- **get extra educational "mileage" out of special occasions.**

You may want to give some thought to the "whys" as you consider the "hows" of getting students to "take the reins." You might also think of additional ways to:

OFFER STUDENTS FREEDOM WITH RESPONSIBILITY

What better way is there to teach the fundamentals of our democratic way of life than by having students "live" it as much as possible within their classrooms? According to our survey, the more successful teachers work toward this goal by giving their students:

- more chances to plan and direct activities,
- more freedom of movement and expression,
- more leeway for self-selected endeavors, and
- more involvement in correcting their papers and recording their own progress.

Counterbalancing their greater freedom, of course, is the students' higher degree of responsibility—for themselves and to others. What can *you* do to cultivate this kind of student maturity?

Get students to shoulder some responsibility for their own learning

Wanda Ward's kindergarteners often plan activities *as a group*. Her young students make thoughtful suggestions and decisions about class behavior, field trips, and even some aspects of curriculum and instruction.

Third-graders in Winnefred Haugland's Vermont class are given as much *individual independence* as they can handle. Her students have access to a great variety of books and materials, can change the classroom arrangement for special projects, and may go to other teachers or students for advice or assistance when needed—as long as they handle these privileges well.

Charles Zeichner, an eighth-grade Mathematics teacher, places a chart at the back of his classroom on which students check off accomplishments and completed tasks by themselves. His students also *monitor their own progress* and tell him when they are ready to be tested on a particular skill.

Barbara Webster encourages her junior high school Remedial Reading students to objectively *grade themselves* for reading improvement, reading achievement, and cooperation. Reasons must be given and evidence shown. Her students respond with surprisingly accurate appraisals—and often with an increased desire to achieve more in the future.

Puts sutdents in responsible positions toward others

All of the fourth-graders in Connie Anderson's upper elementary class are taught to be *audio-visual "aides"* at their school. Ms. Anderson sees to it that all students learn to use the machines and equipment, so that they can help her and other teachers as well as themselves. Needless to say, her students are in constant demand!

Joseph Paradise's sixth-graders *plan monthly programs* for their parents. Their agendas may include original displays, dramatizations, student-parent discussions, or other special events centering around their studies.

The *"criticom" sessions* held by Alex Dobrowolski's junior high school classes turn students into serious evaluators of each other's efforts. During these open discussions, compliments as well

as criticism are exchanged. (Thus they are called "criti . . . -com . . ."
sessions.)

Going a step further, Wally Bain uses a variety of *student-response forms*, like the one in Exhibit 9-1, to encourage his high school Science students to evaluate both teaching methods and curriculum. "The kids really enjoy helping me out in this way, and their input is invaluable to me for my future planning," says Mr. Bain.

Helen Tieger gives her junior high school students the greatest of all responsibilities: *teaching* other students and classes! Her students plan lively ways to share their newly acquired knowledge and, in small groups called "roving troupes," make scheduled presentations to those who are interested in their topics.

KEEP CONTACT WITH INDIVIDUALS WITHOUT LOSING GROUP COHESION

Top-notch teachers are masters at keeping in close touch with individual students and, simultaneously, fostering group rapport. How do they manage it? They:

Schedule highly motivating student-teacher conferences

Nancy Tompkin's students excitedly work toward informal *talk sessions* during which student and teacher together scrutinize progress charts—and enthusiastically plan for developing any interests, and meeting any needs, that "crop up."

Edwin R. Mitchell invites his students to *"Let's Chat Conferences"* to give them a chance to tell him about their independent reading, on a one-to-one basis. They enjoy these so much that they very naturally increase their outside reading activities, which in turn sharpen their in-school efficiency.

Barton L. Kline's students respond to his *"inquiry approach"* with a more energetic involvement in their studies. At a private student-teacher rendezvous, the teacher acts as a benevolent interrogator, and the student gives a personal accounting of accomplishments.

Jane Brake finds that conferences with her students are a good way to *keep lines of communication open* and can make a great difference in student attitude and achievement. She uses these opportunities to get students to express their feelings and to give some serious thought to the practicality of what they are learning in her English classes. So flexible is her approach that when students are working together on a project or have a common bond she lines up joint "get-togethers," for two, three, or even fifteen students!

**EXHIBIT 9-1: STUDENT RESPONSE FORM FOR
BIOLOGICAL SCIENCE**

1. How much did you enjoy taking this course?
   VERY LITTLE   LITTLE   SOME
   MUCH   VERY MUCH

2. How much did you learn?
   VERY LITTLE   LITTLE   SOME
   MUCH   VERY MUCH

3. How would you rate the instructor of this course?
   VERY POOR   POOR   FAIR
   GOOD   EXCELLENT

4. To what extent do you feel you got individual help?
   VERY LITTLE   LITTLE   SOME
   MUCH   VERY MUCH

5. How has the course affected your attitude toward
   the subject area studied?
   LIKE MUCH LESS   LESS   SAME
   MORE   MUCH MORE

6. You were allowed to work at your own rate of
   speed; how did you like this?
   VERY LITTLE   LITTLE   SOME
   MUCH   VERY MUCH

7. What part of the course did you like best?
   READING   LAB   OPTIONAL WORK
   OTHER _____

EXHIBIT 9-1 (continued)

8. After having paced yourself in your learning, to what extent do you feel able to organize and be responsible for your own activities?

   VERY LITTLE   LITTLE   SOME

   MUCH   VERY MUCH

9. If you could start over in this course, what one thing would you do differently? _____

10. To what extent do you feel this course has prepared you for other science?

    VERY LITTLE   LITTLE   SOME

    MUCH   VERY MUCH

11. What additional comments do you have? Use reverse side if necessary.

Utilize the dynamics of class meetings

While private conferences promote student participation on a more individual basis, class meetings can get the entire group into the act.

Full-class meetings are strongly recommended in William Glasser's *Schools Without Failure,* the educational book which has been the greatest inspiration to the greatest teachers (see Chapter 2). According to Dr. Glasser, class meetings are occasions for *nonjudgmental discussions* about issues and ideas that are important and relevant to the students. These may center around a student or class problem, a thought-provoking topic, or a study-related matter.[1]

When Jane Manzelli's sixth-graders meet as a group, they sit in a circular pattern in an area about one-fourth the size of the classroom. They talk about concerns, discuss books, or put on impromptu *dramatic presentations* in this "theatre in the round."[2]

For Brenda Pena's class, meetings are not a formal part of the school day, but just "happen" whenever they are needed or desired. When they do, the students themselves take charge and openly exchange ideas regarding an assembly program, a class trip, *plans* for a party, or just about anything!

During Margy Nurik's *"buzz sessions,"* students have a chance to air complaints, voice criticisms, or offer controversial opinions. Some valid objections which were presented at these times have resulted in sound solutions, such as the extension of a project deadline which came too close to a test day and the adoption of a weekly "free time" period for students to do work of their own choosing.

In Mary Ann Brady's classes, students choose class officers, and even devise their own constitution. They learn a great deal about the American way of life at these *formal meetings* and, at the same time, get totally involved in setting up guidelines and making decisions related to their own education.

USE REINFORCERS TO HELP STUDENTS DEMAND THE BEST OF THEMSELVES

Positive incentives—rewards and awards—are used much more by outstanding teachers than by their more average colleagues. The following strategies, which they have found effective, may be worth a try in your classroom:

Use tangible forms of recognition

Carolyn C. Haines uses original *certificates* of merit in conjunction with a commercial reading program. She noticed that her elementary students needed more acknowledgments than the program provides; so she designed forms with spaces for achievements and completion dates. Her certificates also show the name of the student and the school, and they are signed by both her and the principal.

A Physical Education teacher, Michael Mason, finds that his elementary students get very excited about his dittoed *trophy picture*, shown in Exhibit 9-2. These are awarded not only for feats like skipping rope 200 times in succession or "sinking" ten out of fifteen throws at the basket, but also for creative accomplishments like interpreting music with movement, creating fitness exercises, or finding the most ways to propel a ball.

Lynn Lothian likes to reinforce positive behavior and exceptional efforts in fun ways; so she uses lots of *spur-of-the-moment surprises* to delight her primary students. She may draw a funny cartoon on an outstanding paper, chalk a star onto a child's forehead, or let a student watch as she quickly makes an attractive badge to be worn proudly.

Make-believe money worked wonders for Emily Ehm's uppergraders during their five-week study of careers. Student-selected

EXHIBIT 9-2: TROPHY PICTURE

assignments were "paid" with this currency so eager students could "purchase" anything from a grade to an actual day of work at a local business or store. According to Ms. Ehm, the "budget-minded" students worked twice as hard as usual—and enjoyed it ten times more!

Offer honors and privileges as incentives

Shirley Johnson's high schoolers may be rewarded with some *free time* in the classroom; Lita Grabeklis' students may get to accompany her to *special events* either in or out of school; and Shirley Moore's students may *choose an enjoyable activity,* like applying their Math and Reading to cooking something yummy!

Lettie Siddens motivates her students to do their best by setting up an appealing *bulletin board display* featuring the children's favorite storybook characters. This is a place of honor for the "best paper yet" from each student; it encourages children to "outdo themselves" rather than competing with others.

I have used the technique of offering tickets to qualified students for the privilege of attending *special class functions* (student-planned activities, guest speaker appearances, field trips, etc.). Tickets could be obtained by successfully completing tasks related to recent studies or to the rewards themselves. For example, in order to hear a visitor from the Lost Pet Service, a student might do one of the following:

- name and describe four classifications of animals,
- read a chapter about animals in a Science textbook,
- list four good questions for the speaker, or
- present an animal poem or story to the class.

Additional ways to earn tickets could be suggested by individuals, but would have to be approved at a class meeting. This ticket technique never failed to attract an all-out student effort and invariably added that extra "spark" to both the students and the impending event.

Plan activities with intrinsic rewards

Activities which capture student interest and enthusiasm are often rewards in themselves. Marie Hanlon's fifth-graders, for example, put out a monthly *newspaper* containing articles, research reports, student-devised contests, and creative writing. The joy of seeing their periodical sent out to all schools in town was ample payment for their hard work.

The same children also took part in a school-wide *planting project.* Each grade was in charge of planting a row in what became a fertile 15x20-foot garden of tomatoes, eggplants, pepper, and squash. Much incidental learning took place as the students cared for their plants—and much satisfaction was felt as they reaped the "vegetables" of their labors.

The prospect of a *"Day of Silence"* captivated the imagination of Emily Ehm's English students—especially because sponsors agreed to make a contribution to the local youth bureau for each minute of silence. Her classes responded with a host of creative ideas for worthwhile quiet activities ("say it in writing" situations, "pantomime-to-paper" stories, "read to learn" assignments, etc.). And their enthusiastic cooperation raised more than $1,000 in donations.

Ann Zuzov's elementary students were no less than ecstatic when they learned that through their *lobbying* New Jersey had gained a state insect. Their research uncovered the need and pointed to the honeybee as the most deserving candidate. An assemblyman visited the class and was so impressed that he introduced the bill for them.

An intensive petition drive for signatures, a research report with paintings and drawings, letters to influential people and other classes for support, and the study of how a bill is passed were also part of this unforgettable learning experience. When the Assembly Committee met, Ms. Zuzov and four costumed "bees" attended. After a poem and song were presented the vote was taken—and a unanimous "yes" was proclaimed for the honeybee!

MAKE THE MOST OF SPECIAL OCCASIONS

Are birthdays and holidays recognized in *your* classroom? If so, you are joining ranks with A+ Teachers because they plan more occasion-related activities than Other Teachers. They find unique and exciting ways to:

Capitalize upon the "magic" of birthdays

How can you make student birthdays an enjoyable and memorable part of the school experience? Consider the following:

- Ruth Townsend writes *poems* for birthday children.
- Janet L. Ryan gives her kindergarteners a handmade birthday crown, a balloon, a lollipop, and a chance to relate exciting *birthday news* to the class.
- Alice Kihn's students get a birthday banner which hangs all day in their classroom in their honor—and they are permitted to bring *treats* for the class.
- *"Pupil of the Day"* is the title bestowed upon birthday people in Gloryl Parchert's class, along with privileges like delivering messages and choosing special activities.
- In my classroom a monthly bulletin board displays "profiles" of children whose birthdays are due. To secure pertinent data, students are asked to complete the *special information sheet* shown in Exhibit 9-3 at the beginning of the school year, and to "update" it on their birthdays.

EXHIBIT 9-3: BIRTHDAY INFORMATION SHEET

(Student snapshot)

HAPPY BIRTHDAY, *Donna*

IMPORTANT INFORMATION

Birthdate (and Year) _____

Height at start of school year _____

Height on birthday _____ Inches gained _____

Number of brothers _____ Sisters _____

Pets _____

Favorites:

    Color _____

    TV program _____

    Game _____

    Place _____

    Season _____

    Food _____

    School subject _____

    Holiday _____

    "Happy thought" _____

In our survey, one high school teacher questioned the appropriateness of celebrating birthdays during, for example, a Chemistry class. Perhaps it does have a humorous ring, yet some of the best junior and senior high school teachers do indeed recognize student birthdays:

- Josephine J. Owen places a *paperback book* in the desk of a birthday child in her junior high school English classes, along with a little card.

- Donovan J. Holderness sees that birthdays are acknowledged in his high school Typing and Shorthand classes. Student-planned *bulletin boards* incorporate birthday wishes—written in shorthand or neatly typed, of course!

- A *"Happy Birthday Everybody"* party fills the bill for Margaret J. Rourke's Home Economics students. On these special occasions much of what the students have learned is put to the test as they plan a menu to celebrate each others' birthdays.

- John M. Selig challenges his high school Mathematics students with *birthday Math.* He may, for example, ask the students to find out the probability of two students having a birthday on the same day. Since there is roughly a ½% chance of this occurring, such an event is generally celebrated with an extra-enjoyable class activity.

Put other special occasions to good educational use

Holidays and other special occasions may hold just as much fascination for your students as birthdays do. You may do well not to compete with these outside diversions but, instead, to benefit from them, skillfully weaving them into your plans.

Sarah Schreiner's students enjoy many *special activities* related to holidays and other occasions. Her kindergarteners make cookies for visiting parents during Education Week, have an egg hunt at Easter time, and enjoy a taffy pull, an apple bob, a pumpkin seed roast, and a Jack-o-lantern parade on Halloween. For April Fool's Day, Mrs. Schreiner suggests "gags" like this one:

> Take an old plastic dish detergent bottle containing a screw-on top with a hole. Put a string through the hole and knot it on both ends. Pull the entire string into the bottle until stopped by the knot—and screw the top on. To surprise students, just press the bottle and there'll be lots of excitement as the string (rather than soap as expected) sprays out!

Jean D'Arcy Maculaitis' foreign-born students learn about each others' native land by *discussing ethnic holidays* at the appropriate times; Edward Helwick's high school students present *original dramas* to commemorate highlights like "Bill of Rights Day"; and Margaret J. Payne's students design *bulletin board displays* encompassing noteworthy occasions and historical events.

Barbara Webster uses holidays as themes for *games* like "Password," which help her students concentrate on educational activites even though they are excited about forthcoming celebrations.

Carolyn C. Haines' first-graders make a prose and poetry booklet entitled "What Is a Mother?" for an annual *Mother's Day Luncheon.* They also prepare food and entertainment for their guests of honor.

Another teacher, Hazel Goldstein, makes *the last day of school* very special by telling her students that all work done on this day will be forwarded to their next year's teacher. Time flies by as students review the curriculum and prepare exemplary samples of their work. Mrs. Goldstein not only sees to it that the new teacher gets these papers, but suggests that he or she return them with positive and encouraging comments at the beginning of the new term.

* * * * * *

What students are told or shown seldom nourishes their minds and souls as much as that which they themselves learn or discover. With this in mind, the most effective teachers find a multitude of ways to get their students to become more actively involved.

They delegate more freedom and responsibility to the class and to individuals. Guidance is provided and communication maintained through class meetings and private conferences. Extra "drive" is given to students through rewards and recognitions, along with observance of important occasions. The goal? To make students confident, capable, "high gear" learners!

* * * * * *

10 EXPANDING STUDENT HORIZONS WITH THE HELP OF OTHERS

As one person, no matter how capable and conscientious you are, you simply cannot "do all" and "be all" for your students. To attempt this is to place excessive demands upon yourself and to deprive your students of some very exciting and enriching learning experiences.

As we "tune in" on this mother-daughter dialogue, take note of the great variety of people who can help you and, at the same time, inspire your students!

Mother: (looking at a notice from her daughter's kindergarten teacher): Would you like me to come and help out at school once a week, Beth?

Beth: Oh, yes, Mom! Billy's mother comes, and so does Mary's, sometimes.

Mother: What do the mothers do?

Beth: They read stories or help us learn our colors—or just about anything!

Mother: You have a wonderful teacher, Beth. Do you think she really needs my help? She already has help from the Art teacher, the Music teacher, the Gym teacher, and the librarian, right?

Beth: Our *teacher* doesn't need you—the kids do! When mothers and fathers come in, it's really "neat." Joan's father came in last week to tell us about his job—he's a policeman.

Mother: Miss Logan, the teacher's aide, helps too, doesn't she?

Beth: Uh-huh, and sometimes bigger kids come in to show us something or put on a program for us. Yesterday Mr. Bailey came, and we talked about winter coming. He showed us pictures of how some animals live in winter.

Mother: Mr. Bailey, the *principal?*

Beth: Yes! And we even have a man and lady from college that help sometimes. So don't worry, Mom, you won't be the only helper. Please come!

According to our survey, outstanding teachers do *not* monopolize their students. On the contrary, the most successful ones are far more likely to seek out others to take part in teaching, or working with, their students.

In this chapter you will find a large selection of tested ideas to help you:

- get your principal into the act,
- utilize "parent power,"
- make the most of volunteer assistance, and
- reap the benefits of the usual, and some of the unusual, helpers.

A teacher's most valuable outside assistance generally comes from teachers of special subjects (Reading, Physical Education, Mathematics, Art, Science, etc.) within the school. Top-rated teachers do not stop there, however, but seek out other capable and interested people. Thus, they recommend that you, too:

GET YOUR PRINCIPAL TO "WORK FOR YOU"

Have you ever tried "inverse delegation"—getting your boss to lend *you* a helping hand in the classroom? Why not tap this resource once in a while? Many of the best teachers are getting some valuable professional aid from their principals because they encourage and invite it!

Be open to your principal's inclinations to help

When principal Stephen Shea offered to *teach golf* to interested kindergarten students, the teacher responded enthusiastically and saw that participating students kept their "dates" with him. She was glad she did, because she noticed:

1. An improvement in the students' coordination, which is an educational "plus" for learning the basic academic skills,

2. A higher student self-image and a hearty appreciation of the sport,

3. An increased interest on the part of the principal in further direct involvement with her students.

As director of the school-wide Learning Center, Lola Lehman welcomes the assistance of her principal, whom she refers to as her "right hand." When the center gets over-crowded, as it often does, the principal steps right in to *teach academics* or help students locate materials, prepare reports, and set up displays or equipment.

Rinna Wolfe is another teacher who makes productive use of her principal's desire to maintain direct contact with students. Because her principal often expresses a sincere interest in what students accomplish in class, she encourages them to send him poems, works of art, and exceptional papers. He proudly *displays student work* on his door, and all who pass by see that here is something of value and someone who cares—a very positive influence on attitudes *and* schoolwork.

Also try requesting principal assistance

Harold Cotler's principal not only assists in developing curricular materials (his own idea) but also occasionally enlivens History lessons with his profound knowledge of, and enthusiasm for, the subject (Mr. Cotler's idea). As a *guest speaker,* the principal comes equipped with a collection of old history books dating back to the Civil War and a variety of authentic Colonial antiques. He leaves having ignited a similar interest and enthusiasm in the students.

Russell Nelson's principal is not only an excellent administrator who inspires a dynamic faculty and successful educational programs, but is also a gifted *instructor*—a talent Mr. Nelson does not overlook! He describes his principal as "a photography buff and an excellent graphic artist"; so when such assistance is needed, guess who is on the agenda!

Elsie Hart's principal readily responds to an invitation to visit her classroom. He generally ends up telling a story, teaching a special lesson, or just enjoying some *informal interaction* with the students.

High school principals, too, can be most agreeable. Clara Humphrey's is delighted to act as a *vocational consultant* to her English classes, inviting interested students to his office to discuss a variety of occupations, including his own.

Even *superintendents* will sometimes step into a teacher's "shoes." District superintendent Carl Padovano plans a yearly History unit with high school teachers, then helps to implement it.

STEER PARENTAL INTEREST INTO PRODUCTIVE CHANNELS

Parental assistance need not be limited to the typical field trip and party chaperoning, annual fund-raising, and the like. Consider some of the "parent potential" which has already been discovered:

Behind-the-scenes assistance

Students at Bank Street School in New York City enjoy a creative and durable *play area,* designed and built by their parents. In Stamford, Connecticut, parents constructed raised platforms with stairways and railings in some classrooms as *"reading lofts"* or "retreats." They also made shelves, room dividers, and other useful additions.

A talented mother of one of Chris Sabo's second-graders brightened up the school corridor by painting a *mural* depicting a favorite children's poem. Other parents help out by preparing *educational games* either using their own ideas or following a given plan.

Diane Mazzei gratefully accepts parents' offers to type and mimeograph *worksheets* for classroom use. Art teacher Gary C. Rhiel gets parents into the act by soliciting *donations* of twine, wood, and other media for student projects—and he gets an excellent response!

In-the-classroom aid

Parents assist Marie Hanlon, a fifth-grade teacher, by *helping students* on an individual basis, checking papers for and with them, and sharing special knowledge or talents with the entire group.

The mother of one of my third-graders had an exceptional talent for sewing. When asked to give us some basic instruction on how to use our new sewing machine, acquired through a "Technology for Children" program, she was pleased to do it. She then continued to help us by *advising* and assisting small groups of students each time we planned a sewing project.

Parents also enjoy *taking part in special activities.* Edwin R. Mitchell used parents' culinary skills for a multi-ethnic dinner during which students learned about dishes representative of various countries. A spread of international cuisine, coupled with parent's explanations of their contributions, made this a most satisfying experience in more ways than one!

Shirley Johnson involves parents in *repairing equipment* used by her high school Physics students, thus enabling the school to avoid costly repair bills. The best part, however, is when the parent invites the class to watch the completion of the repair job and provides information that the properly working instrument would never have offered!

At-home help

An educational Gallup Poll showed that 59% of American adults believe that the quality of education is declining due to parent's lack of concern and supervision.[1] Another poll showed that the vast majority of parents are actually anxious to help their children and would like to take a course to learn how to assist them with schoolwork.[2] It is to everyone's advantage, therefore, to get parents educationally involved.

Letha Kemp Smith does this by sending parents a *monthly newsletter* outlining school activities and listing specific ways to help their children at home.[3]

A Brookfield, Connecticut, school uses *parent conferences* to elicit parental aid. When Janet Carney attends a school conference, her daughter Kim accompanies her. All three parties (parent, teacher, and student) plan in writing what active part they will take during the coming semester to make it a successful one.

Doris Kneppel implemented *parent-child partnerships* to improve the reading skills of her second-graders. She instructed parents in phonetic principles, supplied them with individualized prescriptions for their children, and gave them tips on how to make this joint effort enjoyable and productive. These "parent teachers" kept in close touch with her throughout the semester, and final evaluations showed that the children gained eleven month's growth in vocabulary and nine month's in comprehension—in just five month's time!

Elsie F. Hart created a *"Make-It—Take-It" Workshop* which also enlisted parents as at-home helpers. Meeting with her in June prior to the school year, parents made and used manipulative materials to prepare their children for kindergarten. "Numbers," "Letters," "Colors," "Shapes," and other card series were prepared and put into attractive packets for use during the summer. Included in each packet were written instructions like those in Exhibit 10-1. This approach paid such educational dividends that Ms. Hart is now conducting similar workshops throughout the school year.

**EXHIBIT 10-1: PARENT "MAKE-IT—TAKE-IT"
INSTRUCTION SHEET**

This packet teaches children to observe differences in what they see, thus strengthening their "visual perception skills." Please use this packet with your child in the following manner:

1. Arrange cards in a row, making one card face a different way.

   → ↑ → →

   Ask, "Which one is different?"

2. Arrange cards so that just two cards face the same way.

   ↑ → ← ↑

   Ask, "Which ones look the same?" and "Which ones are different?"

3. Make additional design cards of your own. Some suggestions are:

   | d | d | d | b | | w | w | m | w |

   | c | cc | c | c | | | n | s | z |

VIP's (Very Involved Parents) in Chicago helped their underachieving children by:

- providing them with good "basics" such as proper food and clothing, and a well-lighted study area at home.
- reading to them often and helping them think well of themselves.
- seeing that they attend school regularly, then doing special "homework" with them and complimenting them for even minor achievements.

Both parents and children signed contracts pledging to do their part to the best of their abilities. The result? These same students are now reading up to, and above, national levels, more than doubling the gains of those not in the program—something which the classroom teacher alone could not have accomplished![4]

OPEN NEW VISTAS FOR, AND WITH, VOLUNTEERS

Not all teachers are fortunate enough to have paid helpers, but all teachers *can* enlist volunteers, on a regular, occasional, or one-time basis. Education is third only to the health and religious fields when it comes to the utilization of volunteers[5] —and the top teachers, especially at the elementary levels, readily seek them out. You, too, can . . .

Draw volunteers into your classroom

Former students, home from college for vacation, sometimes visit Charles Hoyt's Advanced Biology classes to explain or supervise during lab periods.

Retired teachers teach, tutor, or just help out in Clara Humphrey's high school English classes. Their professional skills, and the students' awareness that they are there solely because they care, have made a noticeable difference in both academics and attitudes.

In Sharon A. Watson's kindergarten, *senior citizens* help out by teaching crafts, reading to students, sharing hobbies, or displaying their unique skills. The appreciative youngsters love them like their own grandparents.

To enrich her high school Spanish classes, Charlene Hickey invites *local residents* who know the language to serve as conversation catalysts or to help with projects for the Spanish Club.

In Monroe Township, N.J., a wealth of community volunteers are available to the schools through a semi-annual program called *"Operation Gold Rush."* The gold is in what the volunteers have to offer as they explain their jobs, discuss their travels, or give specialized instruction—and the rush is on as soon as current listings are distributed to the teachers![6]

Venture out for volunteers

Russell Nelson highlights his study unit on Television Production by bringing his junior high school students to a *nearby college* where they discuss their subject with a real "pro" who teaches graduate students. Here they also learn video-taping techniques in a well-equipped studio.

Mike Ford takes his eighth-graders on *archeological expeditions* when studying early Americans. He arranges for volunteers from the Oregon Archeological Society to prepare "digs" and assist in identifying any "finds". The thrill of working with these experts leaves many of his students with a desire to pursue their interest further, even to the point of joining the society.

Emily Ehm often sends her students on *interviewing excursions,* with questionnaires and tape recorders, to extend their classroom studies. Parents, community workers, college personnel, and local authorities in specialized fields are happy to volunteer as interviewees.

Donovan J. Holderness sends his Typing and Shorthand students out into real-life situations on *"Secretarial Visitation Days"* during which they are given actual work experience by interested businesses. His students return to class with exciting stories, a renewed appreciation of the practical value of their schoolwork, and sometimes even attractive job offers.

GET HELP FROM UNEXPECTED SOURCES, TOO!

Excellent teachers are the first to admit their limitations—and the first to engage others to "fill the gaps." Harry H. Koch, for example, teaches four major and three minor subjects, along with a variety of elective courses in Science and Mathematics. Yet, when he alone cannot adequately answer student questions or provide the necessary guidance, he readily finds someone who can.

Our survey shows that the best teachers get more help than Other Teachers—because they warrant it *and* seek it. You, too, can put others' time and talents to good educational advantage if you . . .

Don't overlook the obvious

Have you considered arranging to have *future teachers* train with you? Top-rated teachers, especially, take advantage of this opportunity and find it to be a valuable experience for all concerned.

Some teachers also corner *college students* specializing in law, medicine, social work, science, etc. as guest speakers, consultants, field trip guides, and the like. William F. Higdon, for example, singles out those who have lived or traveled in foreign countries to add authenticity to his Geography classes.

Part- or full-time aides are also used largely by superlative teachers. These assistants work hard to help your students learn and to help you teach more effectively. Don Gibson's aide helps with record-keeping, and Barbara E. Carlson's is a "partner" in a successful disciplinary approach. Whenever one of her Special Education students misbehaves, either she or her aide displays the firmness needed to rectify the situation, while the other displays gentleness and approachability—a winning combination!

Substitute teachers are in a strategic position to help, but can do so only in proportion to the "tools" given to them. One highly acclaimed teacher recommends making a list of important details for substitutes and leaving a "substitute's folder" containing activities that will be a "hit" with students and fill a curricular goal at the same time.

In Hillsdale, N.J., workshops are offered periodically to familiarize substitute teachers with responsibilities and procedures. A discussion of common problems and an exchange of practical teaching ideas also takes place.

Look in less obvious places, too

We have discussed principals as teachers and parents as teachers; so how about trying *students* as teachers? A study of fourth-graders showed that children who conferred with peers during an assignment learned more than those who did their work without peer interaction.[7]

Knowing that students do indeed learn a great deal from each other, elementary teacher Janet L. Ryan and high school teacher Clida Hunter use both formal and informal *peer teaching* within their classrooms.

Lois K. Smith encourages a beneficial student "give and take" by having her elementary students design some classwork themselves. Exhibit 10-2 is a sample of a worksheet created by one of her students to review subtraction with "borrowing." The egg-laying theme was chosen because the class was also involved in a study of chickens. The child prepared the ditto, explained it to the class, assisted peers when necessary, and later led the follow-up discussion.

EXHIBIT 10-2: STUDENT-PLANNED WORKSHEET

Cross-age interaction can also be beneficial. Several fifth-graders spend much of their lunch hour working with Ann Koprowicz' kindergarteners—helping them with coats and boots, playing games with them, and guiding their reading and writing practice. The sincere interest of these upper-grade friends has had a noticeable effect on the social, emotional, and academic growth of their younger charges.

In the Bronx, N.Y., older students having trouble with reading were given the responsibility of helping younger students with similar problems, on a one-to-one basis. They were very understanding "teachers," especially enthusiastic in a role generally awarded to superior students. Results of the experiment showed that not only did the younger ones gain from the experience, but the tutors

themselves made even greater gains—some achieving more than two years' growth in less than a year![8]
Other less obvious helpers may include:

- *Teachers on educational television.* Doris Turner expresses pure gratitude to a TV Science teacher for giving her students experiences with scientific equipment and procedures which she could never offer.

- *"Amity Aides."* Charleen Hickey reminds us to be on the lookout for organized programs, like this one which places qualified people from all parts of the world in classrooms of foreign language teachers.[9]

- *The school secretary,* cafeteria personnel, and other school workers. So positive and far-reaching was the influence of a female custodian in a Texas elementary school that the new high school was named in her honor—for her eighteen years of "specialized attention" to the students.[10]

- *The people closest to you.* Some of the best teachers credit understanding families or very patient spouses for their encouragement, support, and school-related assistance.

Ann Koprowicz manages to get just about everyone who enters her kindergarten classroom involved with her insatiable learners. By encouraging *visitors* to openly respond to student questions and assist in their work, she turns them into very willing "extemporaneous educators."

Going even farther, Gil Marshall tries to make his students aware of that limitless and fascinating resource he himself constantly uses, and which he hopes they, too, will appreciate: "literally *the entire world of people."*

* * * * * *

Who, then, aside from you, can help to expand your students' horizons? In-school specialists are universally helpful. But, like the A+ Teachers interviewed, you may find that classroom aides, college interns, parents, principals, volunteers of various types, and a host of others can also play a part in making yours a richer, broader, and more effective educational program.

* * * * * *

11 MINIMIZING AND DEALING WITH THOSE BOTHERSOME DISCIPLINE PROBLEMS

Why do A+ Teachers have fewer discipline problems than Other Teachers? Many of them ardently affirm that they have none at all!

The difference lies not in the problems students bring to class; teachers have little or no control over these. The answer is found in what these top teachers do in their classrooms to re-direct or eliminate counter-productive behavior patterns. Here are two teachers discussing this very topic now:

Teacher 1: How do you do it? I never see your students at Mr. Sterns office—and I hardly ever see parents of your students being summoned to school. But I know you have some notorious problem students in your classes.

Teacher 2: Well, for one thing, I *plan* for fewer discipline problems just as I plan to cover certain material.

1: Those plans are worth a million! What do they contain?

2: It's not something that can be patented. Like everything else in teaching, methods differ from teacher to teacher and class to class. Part of my planning is to check my own procedures to be pretty sure that *I'm* not responsible for boredom or frustration, which can trigger problems.

1: You mean that you take a good look at your teaching strategies, materials, and things like that?

2: Sure! You'd be surprised how many problems need not occur at all. I also read books, take courses, and find better ways to respond to tough situations so that my attitudes and reactions won't make things even worse.

MINIMIZING DISCIPLINE PROBLEMS

1: I've seen you giving students little signals in the auditorium. I give a lot of small reminders too.

2: Yes, often these little messages are all that is needed to dissipate minor annoyances.

1: Do you ever have private little talks with problem students like I do?

2: Certainly, but then I try not to lecture or moralize. Instead, I try to shift the responsibility to them. After all, they'll be facing problems throughout their lives; so they may as well learn how to work out their own solutions now. Sometimes the entire class will help out. You'd be amazed at the mature assistance they can provide.

1: What about punishment? Do you ever give extra assignments, deprive a student of a field trip, or yell at a kid in front of the class?

2: I try not to. It usually only causes bitterness between the student and myself—and why should I suffer? I'm generally not even part of the incident or problem. By keeping my own emotions away from the disciplinary situation, I am in a much better position to help students, whose emotions are probably *not* under control.

1: You've given me some good ideas.

2: I have some books you may find helpful, too.

1: Thanks a lot. Let's talk again soon.

Teacher 2 obviously spends more time teaching and less time disciplining. But it doesn't just "happen" that way. This fictional dialogue points out the major disciplinary measures taken by outstanding teachers to make their classrooms as problem-free as possible.

This chapter will show how you, like A+ Teachers, can have an effective disciplinary climate in your classroom by:

- finding more productive alternatives to punishment,
- inviting class assistance in solving behavior problems,
- encouraging students to work out their own problems as much as possible, and
- doing *your* part to "set the scene" for desirable student behavior.

AVOID HAVING TO RESORT TO PUNISHMENT

While A+ Teachers are *more* likely to use positive incentives like the rewards and awards we discussed earlier, they are *less* likely to use negative deterrents, especially punishment. They do not send their students to the principal, seek the assistance of the school disciplinarian, or contact parents as often as Other Teachers do. They much prefer to spend their time and effort encouraging, rather than discouraging, their students.

Is this the most productive attitude to take? Research would appear to indicate that it is. Consider some of the evidence against the "negative approach":

1. A teacher who uses rough, angry words, displays frequent negative emotions, and handles children abruptly actually causes further *anxiety* and misbehavior not only in receivers but also in observers of such treatment.[1]

2. A punished student may escape into daydreaming or *truancy*. He or she may even find the negative attention a rewarding incentive to increase the undesirable behavior.[2]

3. Students of a punitive teacher display more *hostility*, more confusion about behavior standards, and less concern about learning or other positive types of school activities. On the other hand, children with non-punitive teachers are better able to identify with school and accept, even adopt, its values.[3]

Not surprisingly, many teachers in our survey find success with a variety of *strategies which exclude punishment,* such as:

- *Confronting the child* (or the class) with the problem and searching for reasons and productive changes together (Gil Marshall).

- Presenting the child with a *fair choice* regarding behavior, then assisting him or her in accepting the responsibility for living up to that choice (Lillian Flanagan).

- Having two arguing students tell their sides of the disagreement, then *rephrasing* both descriptions. ("We now know that John gets extremely angry when people call him names, and Bill likes to hear an apology if he is pushed accidentally. Am I right?") This alone will often satisfy both, and settle the argument without reprimands or punishment (Margaret Simpson).

- Setting up a student-selected *classroom council* for weekly reviews of problems which crop up (Joseph D. Paradise).

- Expressing *disapproval in constructive ways*, drawing attention to something praiseworthy about the student if possible. For example, saying: "Shouting like that can ruin your lovely singing voice" instead of using one of the many negative or derogatory ways to get the student to be less disruptive (Rinna Wolfe).

- Giving problem students plenty of *positive attention*, such as by assigning special responsibilities. A student who feels good himself or herself is seldom a "trouble-maker" (Myrtle Collins).

When they do punish, A+ Teachers generally use *natural consequences or "positive punishment."* Patricia Sink, for example, does not hesitate to ask a student who is cheating to take the test in isolation, a student forgetting a permission slip to miss the trip, or a child writing on the wall to clean it off.

Mary C. Holden may ask disruptive students to help make the school a better place by clearing up litter in the building or playground on their own time. Worthwhile tasks like this enable the situation to end on an "up" note.

A judge in Minnesota tried giving constructive "sentences" (like donating time for a worthy cause or doing a community service) for first-time law-breakers. The result? Only 4% because repeat offenders, compared to the national average of 50%![4]

USE "CLASS POWER" TO HELP MAINTAIN DISCIPLINE

Our survey shows that the most effective teachers are more likely to draw the entire class into the disciplinary scene. You, too, can tap this "peer power" if you:

Draw the class into behavior-related discussions

Maureen Buckmiller's first-graders talk about disciplinary problems during *class meetings*. If two students are involved, they may "talk out" the problem as the class listens (and later helps).

An Illinois teacher has her students plan *skits and plays* in which they act out both appropriate and inappropriate behaviors for class discussion; Connie Anderson takes the role of the *"devil's advocate"* so her students can better understand the importance of the rules they uphold; and Shirley A. Johnson uses a camera to *film discipline problems* (authentic and enacted) for class debates.

Give the class some say in "what goes"

Mary Ann Anthony's kindergarteners help devise simple *class rules,* which are posted in a prominent place along with student illustrations of the desired behaviors.

Nancy Tompkins' first- and second-graders *set up behavior criteria,* and also help to decide if and when deterrents should be used. A problem involving one student is often shared with the class to develop empathy and problem-solving skills.

Students in Helen Tieger's junior high school classes fill in *"group progress reports"* in which they evaluate the class's behavior and discuss deviations from standards that they helped to develop. They also have a part in handling any related discipline problems.

Capitalize upon the dynamics of peer encouragement

Winnefred M. Haugland encourages her third-graders to *react positively to efforts and successes* of problem students; Jane Brake groups her high school students by tables with highly respected *managers* at each to help keep the students "on the right track"; and June Betsworth lessens problems effortlessly with frequent *"cooperation competitions"* in which groups of students vie for the honor of being the "outstanding" or "runner up" teams.

Each student in Donald DeVries' junior high school Science classes is "his brother's keeper" during lab sessions. Problems seldom arise because students themselves will *stop misbehavior* before it "gets off the ground." The sincerity of his reasoning is what makes his "pitch" so effective and compelling:

> I have only one pair of eyes and can only be in one place at a time. Therefore, each of you has a responsibility to each other. You can see what is happening around you and are usually aware of a problem before I am. So, if you see something that is not what is expected, please inform that individual to stop, especially if there is danger involved to the individual or to other students.

It is important to note that *no* teacher in our survey obtained class disciplinary assistance by threatening to punish all for the misdeeds of some. This type of negative, divisive peer *pressure* is avoided in favor of the more uplifting, unifying group *encouragement* which not only reduces misbehavior, but also builds student confidence and self-esteem.

DEVELOP RESPONSIBILITY AND SELF-DISCIPLINE
IN PROBLEM STUDENTS

A similar approach used significantly more by award-winning teachers is having students *work out problems independently.* This also relieves the teacher of the role of "imposer" of discipline, and encourages students to shoulder more of the responsibility themselves.

Harold Cotler finds that many times students can rectify their own problems. These *student solutions* may be quite severe, according to him, but they generally work out very well. As an example, one boy was reported for using unacceptable language on the playground. Rather than scolding him, Mr. Cotler suggested that the student decide what to do himself. Letters of apology were written to the aide and other child involved, and the incident became a "growing" experience rather than a resentment-filled one.

Both Alva Rinehart and Ann Koprowicz encourage two arguing students to *sit down together* and settle their differences. Other outstanding teachers sit down with misbehaving students to personally guide them in setting and attaining realistic goals for themselves. Many use William Glasser's *"Reality Therapy"* approach for this, which means that they:

1. *Get involved with students* in a warm, personal way.

2. *Deal in the present* when a problem occurs, asking "What are you doing?" or "What's happening?"—so students verbalize the problem.

3. *Get students to make value judgments,* with questions like "How does this affect others?" "Is it helpful?" or "What should you be doing?"

4. *Help students make an acceptable plan* for changing undesirable behavior.

5. *Seal agreements* with a handshake, or preferably in writing.

6. *Refuse to discuss excuses* or reasons for not living up to the agreement, asking only: "When will you?"

7. *Issue no punishments* or consequences (with the possible exception of isolating disruptive students temporarily), but patiently and caringly making new plan commitments as often as necessary—until students assume individual responsibility for their behavior.

Dr. Glasser emphasizes that the teacher should not give up on a child, but should be lovingly firm. When the basic needs of love and worth are met because the teacher cares enough to keep trying, the child will take responsibility for his or her actions, and for changing them if necessary.[5]

WARD OFF PREVENTABLE DILEMMAS

Many problems can be "cut off at the pass" by foresight, sensitivity, and good planning. *All* you need to do is . . .

Encourage the behavior you want

What you expect is generally what you get! So, like Faye Shaw, Lillian Flanagan, and countless other great teachers, have *high expectations.* Or, like Carol DeLorenzo, give your students good reputations to live up to and treat them accordingly.

Discipline problems are just about nonexistent in Catherine Murphy's classroom. How does she do it? She credits her high expectations, along with her sincere fondness for the children, her efforts to draw out the best in each student, and her unusual combinations of "gentle firmness" and "flexible routine."

You may also want to consider the following ways to promote decorum:

1. Diversify your program so students can spend their time and energy pursuing *exciting learning experiences* rather than misbehaving. For example, a variety of carefully planned multi-level activities keeps Lyllian Tubbs' students engrossed, motivated, and challenged.

2. *Be an example* to your students. Clida Hunter treats her students with the respect she likes to receive herself. This counteracts student disrespect and rebellion.

3. Get students to focus on their *positive characteristics,* and they will be more apt to display them. An Illinois Teacher of the Year uses activities like this writing assignment:
   "I like myself because I . . ."

4. *Acknowledge progress.* We all need a "pat on the back" once in a while, and it can make a difference in students' behavior, too. Therese Anglin and Mildred Von der Linden get their students to compete with themselves in exhibiting agreed-upon behavior, then acknowledge sincere efforts with

well-placed comments, stars pasted onto attractive cut-outs, or tokens exchangeable for desirable rewards.

5. Give students *something to reach for.* Use the therapeutic value of great thoughts! /

When the behavior of one of her students began to deteriorate, Margaret Petrusich wrote this on the chalkboard:

I would be true for there are those who trust me.
I would be pure for there are those who care.
I would be strong for there is much to suffer.
I would be brave for there is much to dare.

I would be friend to all—the foe, the friendless.
I would be giving and forget the gift.
I would be humble for I know my weakness.
I would look up and laugh, and love, and lift.

(Howard Arnold Walter)

Later she asked the child to write in his own words what the poem meant. He wrote a stirring essay, concluding with "Thank you, Miss Petrusich." She and the child never discussed it, but his behavior showed that the words had made a lasting impression.[6]

Discourage behavior you cannot sanction—but how?

Hand in hand with encouraging good conduct comes the discouragement of the inappropriate behavior. Surveyed teachers agree that it is essential to recognize and encourage good behavior, but appear to be divided in their responses to incorrect behavior. Some teachers have phenomenal success with behavior modification techniques, which completely ignore the behaviors to be eradicated, but many feel that incorrect behavior cannot always (and some feel should *never)* be ignored.

Brenda Pena ties *student accountability* in with self-image when she asks, "Have you ever thought about the self-image you are reinforcing when you do *not* hold students accountable for poor behavior?"

How *can* you show students that you care enough to correct, without accenting the negative too much?

Let them know how you feel. Maxel J. Ferguson and Robert Glover discourage poor behavior by simply making their students aware of their disapproval and disappointment. Studies indicate that *teacher disapproval* is indeed effective—if it is free of threats and coupled with clarifying praise for the proper behavior.[7] When disapproval is expressed through social shaming, sarcasm, or veiled warnings, however, it is more damaging than beneficial.[8]

Give small reminders. But watch your phraseology: be sure to discourage the act and not the person. Reminders like *"You* didn't raise your hand," or *"If you* don't finish . . ."* were found to produce negative results, whereas thoughtful comments that avoid personal offense ("Let's raise our hands before we speak," and *"We* need your finished paper") produced more positive results.[9]

Reprimand clearly yet discreetly. Attitude *and* wording are the keys. One study showed that those comments which defined the problem and specified how to rectify it were most effective.[10] General commands like "Stop it!" may be confusing, whereas clear ones like, "Jeff, please turn around and continue with your written work," have worked well for junior high school Reading teacher, Barbara Webster.

Make some "strategic moves" if necessary. To nip problems "in the bud," Doris Turner may ask disruptive students to go to a special classroom retreat called an *"island"* where they can be by themselves to calm down and think until they are ready to resume their responsibilities.

William Glasser advocates using a desirable and enriching place for this purpose—one with a positive designation, like the classroom *"castle."* Here all students enjoy books, puzzles, educational games, etc., but disruptive students have priority during disciplinary situations. "Castle time" will be well spent, and when the student is ready to return to the group an agreement can be made regarding future behavior.[11]

Be on the lookout for causes and solutions

Frances A. Kiser watches for symptoms, and when her high school students seem inattentive from *sitting too long,* she may provide a change of pace by saying, "OK, everybody up! Walk around the room!" or "Let's take a break for a drink of water." For younger students a short exercise game or other movement activity can revitalize attention spans.

For similar reasons, I found it difficult to keep my third-graders reasonably quiet before school assembly programs began. It was unfair to expect these active children to just sit passively until the program began; so we devised a silent game together which we called *"Creative Daydreaming."* Students (and teacher) relaxed, sat in silence, and put imaginations to work during these "endless" minutes. Back in the classroom, we all felt good about our exemplary behavior—and had fun sharing some of our daydreams!

Teacher-related problems must also be considered because disruptive behavior can most definitely be linked to a teacher's preparation, motivation, and presentation.[1][2] The following are some questions you may want to ask yourself when student behavior is not on "par":

1. *"Am I causing the problem?"*

An elementary Physical Education teacher noticed that some of his colleagues were making disciplinary matters worse by over-reacting, coming to hasty conclusions, being too picayune, or making learning uninteresting. This teacher, therefore, works on his own behavior to make sure that these characteristics do not describe him.

2. *"Are my reactions aggravating the situation?"*

Donna Goldsmith noticed that her reactions were only compounding problems. She realized that if she could have a negative influence, she could also have a positive one. She was right! She now remains "level-headed" during disciplinary situations—and her students have calmed down accordingly!

3. *"Can I make some necessary changes?"*

Hazel C. Morton often looks to her teaching methods when her students' behavior takes a turn for the worse. She may vary routines to be sure that boredom is not the root of the problem. Mrs. Virgil M. Linderoth takes a second look at the work given to a student who is "acting up." Often tasks that are too easy, too difficult, or confusing turn out to be the cause.

Experiment to create a balmier disciplinary climate

Rinna Wolfe has found that *healthful "treats"* help to prevent behavior problems. Her fifth-graders prepare and serve raisins, apples, oranges, and other wholesome foods during special "snack breaks." This practice has the added bonus of teaching social skills and good snacking habits.

Better rapport through *informal interaction* with problem-burdened students works well for junior high school teacher Charles Zeichner. He may, for example, sit down by a child in the lunchroom, speak with him or her on the playground, or use another good opportunity to express the "active caring" which has been instrumental in correcting, and preventing, discipline problems in his classroom.

Private conferences proved to be a popular approach to disciplinary problems for both groups of teachers in our survey. Dorothy A. Jacob culminates hers with the issuance of *contracts* containing workable solutions—signed and monitored by all involved, including the teacher. Another teacher makes her conferences memorable and effective with a *pleasant follow-up activity* such as drawing, painting a mural, or planning a puppet show related to the solution discussed.

National Teacher of the Year Willard C. Widerberg has *group conferences* in which both offenders and victims take part in "healing discussions," and Margy Nurik schedules lunch hour *meetings with interested teachers* (especially those who have worked well with problem students) to get some good ideas for herself. She may also meet with the school psychologist, guidance counselor, principal, and curriculum director to get further suggestions.

Lettie Siddens takes *notes* on problem students to help her pinpoint behavior patterns. When reviewing her notes on Peter, for example, she realized that he visited the lavatory frequently, left work unfinished, and often avoided her. With this written evidence in front of her, the course of action was plain: check out the possibility of a physical problem, see that classwork is challenging but not boring, and try to develop a better rapport. (P.S. He is no longer a problem!)

Finally, two teachers who have found success in this difficult realm of student discipline have graciously volunteered to share their unique systems. It is hoped that you will find their *guidelines* beneficial:

Ellen Silver's "recipe" for good discipline

1. Build positive group norms.
2. Clarify with students what is appropriate behavior.
3. Provide specific feedback to students on their behavior.
4. Develop strategies for dealing with potential offenders.
5. Treat students as individuals—accept differences.
6. Use positive reinforcement.

The "secret formula" used by Donovan J. Holderness

1. Respect students as individuals.
2. Be courteous.
3. Know your subject and be prepared.

4. Exercise your sense of humor.

5. Be tolerant and understanding.

6. Be fair.

7. Be enthusiastic.

Alex Dobrowolski sums it all up like this: "know your subject, know your students, and teach like Hell!" No wonder his discipline problems are few!

*   *   *   *   *   *

You, too, can minimize discipline problems in your classroom if, like the A+ Teachers in our survey, you supplement the usual strategies (private discussions and small reminders) with those that make a difference:

- de-emphasizing punitive approaches, and
- assigning more student responsibility, both individually and as a class.

Add to this your sincere effort to prevent problems, and what will you have? Fewer disruptions, less aggravation and fatigue, more time and verve to teach, happier, more competent students, pleased parents and principal, and job satisfaction!!

*   *   *   *   *   *

12 HOW TO GET STUDENTS TO ACTUALLY CLAMOR FOR HOMEWORK

Do you give homework? To whom? When? Why? What kind?

There are many strong pros and cons on the subject. Not surprisingly, it is considered to be one of the ten major controversial issues in contemporary education.[1]

The practices of our master teachers, however, put homework in a more positive perspective, taking it from its mundane, punitive, enthusiasm-squelching role to where it can do the most good for all involved.

See what differences *you* can pinpoint between the homework policies of these two upper-elementary teachers, who have just finished introducing their students to the art of finding the area of a rectangle:

The first teacher . . .

. . . writes the following instructions on the chalkboard: "Do three rows of problems on page 88 of our Math book; study for a quiz on this tomorrow."

Students are expected to copy, or remember, the assignment and to come into class the next day completely prepared.

The second teacher . . .

. . . puts a pile of mimeographed papers on an empty desk near the door. A colorful sign nearby depicts a well known cartoon character pointing to the stack of papers and saying, "What's up, Doc? Take one and see!"

The paper reads:

"RECTANGLE DAY TOMORROW

Don't be a 'square'—join in the fun.
You may even want to do more than one!

1. Make an illustration showing *why* it is possible to find a rectangle's area in the manner presented in class.

2. Write an original 'story problem' where knowledge gained today is needed to find the solution. Show how the answer can be figured and be ready to challenge the class with your problem.

3. Prepare yourself to explain how to find the area of a rectangle, as if you were going to teach a classmate who missed today's lesson. Include two examples to demonstrate.

4. Show a parent how to find the area of a rectangle, then discuss similarities and differences in how they recall having learned to do it. Be ready to report your findings to us.

5. Find four rectangular items at home. Measure two sides only. Diagram the objects on graph paper, noting the object and the area inside each.

6. Plan a class guessing game. Bring in three rectangular objects for an area estimating contest. Have the exact answers ready.

7. Interview at least two people to ask why it is important in everyday life to be able to figure the area which an object covers. Note the reasons given, with proper credit to each person.

8. Devise your own assignment to make our study today more real, more interesting, or more understandable to yourself or others."

The above situation sheds some light on our survey results regarding homework. The second (A+) teacher will in all likelihood receive at least as much homework on a voluntary basis as the first teacher with mandated homework. *The difference will be that those who do one, or more, of the suggested activities will do so with enthusiasm and self-motivation.* Also, the variety of homework results discussed in class the following day will be a more pleasant and effective way to reinforce the learning than the unimaginative and threatening quiz planned by the first teacher.

> In the following pages, A+ Teachers will show how you can make homework a more desirable and worthwhile enterprise by:
>
> - eliminating many of those boring, sterile assignments,
> - offering students attractive choices for extending their in-school learning,
> - capturing student interest with assignments that are *not* mandatory,
> - planning assignments that will reflect the uniqueness of the doers, and
> - experimenting with new ideas for variety, enjoyment, and student motivation.

If you *always* give homework, you may want to "break free" with some of the flexible approaches to be discussed; if you *sometimes* give it, you may find additional ideas to incorporate; and if you *never* touch it, you just may change your mind! Read and see what *you* think.

WEED OUT ASSIGNMENTS THAT TURN STUDENTS OFF

Statistical results of our survey show that A+ Teachers give significantly fewer *written, textbook, and study assignments.* They eliminate those which are unduly repetitious, vague, or that are just plain "busy work." Assignments like these give the noble, and often necessary undertaking called "homework" a bad name it does not deserve! Home-based learning, especially with parental involvement, can make a vast difference in a student's ability to succed in school.[2]

Do not be misled however, into thinking that quantity is the main consideration. Our survey results show that A+ Teachers actually give less homework. They are concerned with *quality.* So before you "pile it on," ask yourself:

Am I overdoing textbook and workbook assignments?

Too many "set" assignments lead to boredom, copying, and those annoying negative attitudes—and because these are really assignments from the authors of the respective books, they cannot possibly provide for the unique needs of your students *or* yourself. Outstanding teachers, therefore, use them sparingly, often injecting at least a motivating "twist" when they do use them. A page of multiplication problems, for example, may be made more "palatable" when assigned this way:

> *"After completing the problems on page 92:*
> - Find the magic number! Add up all your answers.
> - Challenge your parents to find some answers, without pencil and paper!
> - Check your work with an adding machine or calculator.
> - Devise a dozen more of your own problems (with answers) to be used in class tomorrow."

Are written assignments carefully thought out?

Written assignments are easy to monitor because of the "evidence" they provide that the student (or "someone") has indeed performed the assigned task. They can be very creative and should not be excluded, but if you limit yourself to them, you lose the richness found in other homework activities (reading, dramatizing, making tapes, building models, or just "thinking").

An experiment with fourth-graders showed that there was no advantage to giving students a steady "diet" of written homework assignments.[3] Furthermore, the burden that excessive written duties place upon both the students' and teacher's time often results in loss of enthusiasm and creativity on "both sides of the coin."

To be especially avoided are those which are foisted on students unnecessarily, thoughtlessly, or merely to be discarded without teacher scrutiny. Any of these practices is definitely a teacher "cop-out" and a student "turn-off"! A+ Teachers use the vehicle of writing for creative, challenging, and appealing homework tasks; and you will find many examples as you read through this chapter.

Are my study and preparation assignments confusing?

The all too frequent admonition "Study for the test" is vague and confusing, and it may produce more student anxiety than motivation. A more productive alternative would be to guide students to the desired goal.

For example, instead of just telling students to study for tomorrow's Science test on amphibians, a teacher might prepare, perhaps with class assistance, a *checklist* such as this one:

CHECK YOUR KNOWLEDGE: AMPHIBIANS

Describe the following:

_____ the life cycle of a frog

_____ six examples of amphibians

_____ three distinct characteristics of all amphibians

_____ pre-historic amphibians

_____ man-made amphibious vehicles

This requires the teacher to summarize what the test will cover and helps students to use their study time wisely. A similar structure is equally helpful for preparation assignments not related to tests or quizzes. Rather than telling students to "find leaves" as a follow-up to a Science lesson, the teacher may challenge the class to:

Try to locate:

- a deciduous leaf
- a coniferous leaf
- a leaf which is especially unusual or pretty, to press and preserve
- an oak leaf
- a two-part leaf
- a leaf *we* eat

MAKE STUDENTS AN OFFER THEY CAN'T REFUSE

How do top-rated teachers do this? By giving multi-level, multi-approach, *free-choice assignments* to let students have their say in the what, how, and when aspects of their homework. The more the students can get "into the act," the more meaning homework will hold for them—and the greater their response will be to your homework proposals.

When Special Education teacher Betty B. Willey noticed that the "homework blues" were descending upon her students, she tried a new approach. She gave her elementary students this assignment:

Do something for our study unit on transportation. Be ready to discuss your plan with me.

Ms. Willey permitted each child to choose the preferred mode of transportation and the preferred type of work, be it locating facts, drawing or building something, writing a story, etc. This was a turning point in the students' attitudes toward homework, evidenced not only by their new-found enthusiasm, but also by the unprecedented quality, volume, and variety of the homework they submitted.

In an experiment with an average class, students of Intermediate Algebra were not only actively involved in making their own assignments, but were also allowed to choose when to do them. Given this increased leeway, they responded with more unique, creative, and carefully planned homework assignments. At the same time, both comprehension and independent problem-solving ability surged![4]

Alex Dobrowolski gives his junior high school students choices in how to complete homework. These *open-ended assignments* leave ample room for individual student preferences, initiative, and imagination. When studying land use trends, for example, students were asked to locate information about one square mile of their township. Each student selected a familiar or unknown section of town, and researched whatever aspects most interested him or her.

TAKE STUDENTS FROM APATHY TO
ENTHUSIASM–WITH OPTIONAL ASSIGNMENTS!

A+ Teachers seek to rid their students of homework apathy with the optional assignment, or *homework exclusively for those who want it.* This is the ultimate challenge to the teacher because students will either stop asking for home extensions or merely put "thumbs down" on suggested assignments that are not worthwhile.

Since Sally Hedges changed her mandatory homework policy to an optional one, she reports that her high school students are taking more work home than ever before! And she is giving more thought to devising productive and enticing at-home endeavors which meet the needs and desires of her students.

A *teacher's enthusiasm* is often "catching" and can reinforce students' desire to do more at home. Take, for example, Edith Widicus, who can be aptly described as a reading enthusiast. Her zest for reading has "rubbed off" on her students in a most gratifying way. They spend a great deal of time reading at home–though not formally assigned to do so.

Some teachers have *informal conferences* with interested students to plan rewarding homework. Others try homework boxes, special bulletin board displays, and duplicated listings (like the one at the opening of this chapter) to bring students from grudgingly to willingly to *wholeheartedly* extending their learning beyond the school day.

PUT A CREATIVE FLAIR INTO HOMEWORK

A study of teacher attitudes, policies, and procedures in 77 New York school districts showed that too often students are given identical homework assignments, leaving little space for creativity.[5] "Read Chapter X and answer the questions" may be an acceptable assignment once in a while, but our survey showed that A+ Teachers lean much more toward creative types of homework assignments.

Such assignments may be *"personal prescriptions"* like the ones given by Emily Pritchard Carey. Ms. Carey sees to it that each student has attractive, ever-changing prescriptions, based on individual goals set jointly by student and teacher. Each student proceeds on his or her own material at his or her own rate.

Creative assignments do not have to be equated with individualized assignments, however. The same instructions often result in very original student efforts. Consider the following assignments which were given to the entire class—and also consider the rich variety of homework received.

- *"Prepare three good questions about what we studied today (mammals, England, the five senses, etc.) to be used for a mock TV quiz show tomorrow."*

My elementary students always enjoy such homework assignments, and they often produce far more than requested.

- *"Respond to this question or statement: . . . ,"* or
  "Describe your feelings about . . . ," or
  "Interpret the following: . . . ," or
  "Design a way to . . ."

Eleanor Foley often gives her elementary students tasks like these to do at home. It has been her experience that such assignments elicit superior student responses because they get students to relate to the subject matter in their own unique ways.

- *"Improve the appearance of your home."*

Kay Stapleton's high school Art students enthusiastically look for aesthetic projects that can enhance their home, inside or out. Homework assignments like "Create an artistic rock garden" are carried out with ardor and to the delight, also, of the students' families.

- *"Here's your chance! We need a slogan for the Math Festival. Can you think of one? Deadline Friday."*

Donna Goldsmith draws her junior high school students into creative, at-home involvement by focusing assignments on up-and-coming events, requesting art work, research, learning aids, advertising fliers, bulletin board designs, etc.

- *"Plan a three-dimensional presentation."*

Students in the high school English classes of Frances A. Kiser know what this homework assignment means. The three dimensional aspects are oral, graphic, and creative. A 3-D project about a noted author would entail:

1. a way of telling the class about the author,
2. an exhibit (chart, poster, original transparency, and the like) which can be referred to, and
3. something original: a skit, a mock newscast about the author, an illustrated booklet, a "séance" with the deceased author, or whatever unique approach the student may want to employ.

- *"Write to at least one person whose occupation is particularly appealing to you. Ask questions about his or her work."*

High school students in Jane Brake's classes receive such "minimal assignments," and are invited to go beyond if they desire. They may, for example, write additional letters, conduct personal interviews, or do library research—and many do!

- *"Keep a school diary."*

My third-graders had individual diaries, or notebooks, which they took home each Thursday to record, and perhaps illustrate, highlights of the school week. This provided parents with some answers to the proverbial question, "What are you doing in school?", motivated students to reflect upon what they had learned, and prompted some good follow-up discussions the next day.

- *"Make up a story."*

Kindergarteners in Sharon A. Watson's classes love to get this homework assignment. They plan their stories at home, dictate them to helpful parents or older siblings (who become their "private secretaries"), and often illustrate them for the enjoyment of the entire class.

- *"Bring in something you found or made which relates to our studies, and tell us about it."*

Maralene Wesner uses this as a standard assignment for her kindergarteners. On Fridays each of her students brings in an item that in some way develop the week's theme. It may be a book, a student-made diorama, a clipping, anything! Parents receive an outline of the curriculum as a guide in helping their youngsters to prepare something meaningful for these weekly sessions.

- *"Let's do something different tonight."*

Kathryn Berry looks for enjoyable and unusual homework assignments for her fifth-graders.

She may ask them to devise a time line of significant events in their lives, take a "sound walk" and prepare a checklist of sounds encountered, put together a birthday time capsule to "bury away" at home for three years, or make a class address book.[6]

SPICE IT UP TO INCREASE STUDENT INTEREST

Contrary to widespread practice, Wally Bain encourages his high school Science students to *seek the help of others* (fellow students, parents, experts, and the like) whenever such assistance is beneficial or necessary. This makes homework more exciting and often stretches students' minds. The only stipulation is that these "resources" must be given credit for their contributions.

Lois K. Smith likes to surprise her elementary students with *secret homework sacks.* These contain materials for special at-home experiments. One such assignment provided each student with two pine cones, a cup, and these instructions:

Put water in the cup. Add one pine cone. Wait two hours. Now compare the wet cone to the dry one.

Anne Chatfield's students have special *homework books* in which they record and often do their assignments; Faye Shaw offers an *enjoyable activity* for the entire class when all students fulfill their weekly homework responsibilities; and another teacher sets up a special *honor roll* for students who put forth outstanding efforts after school hours.

Family involvement is another way to make homework more enticing. Maxel J. Ferguson's students often receive the assignment to either teach, or be taught by, someone at home. Another teacher has students make an attractive collection of completed homework assignments to be shared with their families. Some even go so far as to initiate parent-child partnerships like the ones described in Chapter 10.

What is the best way to make student, teacher, and homework a contented threesome? Adherence to the following *guidelines* may not be the whole answer, but they certainly provide six steps in the right direction!

1. Make homework attractive in itself; do not use it for punishment.
2. Try a variety of carefully planned approaches which stimulate, interest, and actively involve your students.
3. Accept student criticism and encourage students to help in planning assignments that are relevant and motivating.
4. Do not let homework make unreasonable demands on students. The *Encyclopedia of Education* suggests the following allotments by grade level (summarized): [7]

Grade	Daily Homework
1	0-10 min.
2-5	15-25 min.
6-8	30-60 min.
9-12	1¼-2 hr.

One high school principal asked parents to observe their children in an experiment during which homework was reduced from three to two subjects and totaled approximately one hour daily (with weekends free). Three-fourths of the parents reported favorable results: noticeably reduced tension and fatigue, increased eagerness, better sleep, and improved general health. Almost 90% of the parents did not want to return to the greater amounts of homework.[8] What percentage of the *students* do you think felt the same way?

5. Be sure to honor student efforts by making thoughtful corrections and evaluations of their homework.

Susan Rosenbluth of the Parent-Child Institute in Fort Lee, N.J., tells of a student who threw her outstanding term paper against the wall in rage. When asked what was wrong, she replied, "I got a lousy A!" She had made a supreme effort, and was frustrated at finding nothing on her paper *but* an A! There was no mention of what was particularly good, what might be done to improve it, etc. In fact, there was no evidence that the teacher had even read it!

So forego the "Very good" and do your students a real service by giving specific feedback like "Superb sentence structure," "Your descriptions of characters are most vivid," "Please review your 9-times table until you know it as well as you know the others," and so on.

6. Put completed homework to additional educational purposes once in a while: display original homework endeavors, set up a learning center in which students can scrutinize and use each other's after-school accomplishments, or have each student keep (and periodically evaluate) his or her own homework log.

*   *   *   *   *   *

Do you give homework? You probably should, in moderation. One study showed that 80% of all students want it—yet 50% feel uneasy about the nature and amount they are receiving.[9]

The best teachers do *not* necessarily give the most homework, but they do give more of the "turn-on" type. This includes assignments for those who want them (and *all* will if it's something exciting!), assignments offering students a say in what will be done, *and* assignments which spark creativity.

Now that you know this secret, you may want to try some of these approaches yourself—and don't be *too* surprised if your students start clamoring for more!

*   *   *   *   *   *

1⒊ TESTING WITHOUT TERRORIZING

What type of reaction does the word "test" evoke in you? A competitive spirit? A rising to the challenge? Pure panic?

In all too many cases, fear *is* the over-riding response, as you may well know from your own experience as a student. And now that you are *administering* tests, what responses are you getting from *your* students? Are they reacting as you once did?

Let's see what opinions the students have to offer as we listen in on an impromptu upper-grade discussion about tests.

Joan: I sure wish we had no tests!

Teacher: Do you think testing serves a purpose?

Billy: Yes, it does. The teacher has to know if we've learned what we were supposed to, and who may need special help, and what marks to give us, too.

Mark: But I once had a teacher who tested us *before* we studied something.

Teacher: Does anyone know what these tests are called? They are called pre-tests. They help the teacher to plan on the basis of what you already know so you won't be bored. And when the same test is used as a post-test at the close of a study, we know how much you have progressed.

Teachers can use tests to check *themselves,* too, you know. Remember that little spontaneous quiz I gave last week on Roman numerals? Well, that was more for me than you. I had tried two very different teaching approaches with my six classes, and by comparing the test scores, *I* learned something too!

Tom: Some teachers are really test-crazy, though! I once had one who gave a test at the close of each session. I think she felt that we wouldn't listen or work hard without that test hanging over us.

151

Teacher: Did that make you work harder?

Tom: Not really!

Teacher: So, what's the verdict? Should I stop giving you tests?

Phil: No, after all, we'll get them in college, so we'd better be prepared.

Joan: We get them outside school too. My sister had to take a test to get a job at the supermarket, and my parents had to study for their citizenship, and *I'm* looking forward to my driver's exam!

Teacher: Well, if we can't eliminate them, how can we improve them?

Joe: I wish teachers would prepare us better by telling us how and what to study, and then testing on *that!*

Mary: I think teachers *should* test us, but tests shouldn't be a major part of grading. I hate to see big exams that count for a whole grade. It's not fair. Some kids take tests better than others, and tests only show a little bit about a person anyway.

Elizabeth: I would like to see fewer pencil-and-paper tests and more imaginative kinds. Maybe you could check our knowledge of Roman numerals by asking us to locate chapters in a book, or design a "way out" clock, or translate a secret Roman code, and things like that.

Ben: I'd like to see test results used for something more than a mark in a gradebook—like earlier this year when we formed those practice teams after that Math test. Those results *showed* us something and helped us all to improve.

Donna: It would be great if we, as students, could have a part in preparing tests sometimes.

Teacher (who has outlined the students' ideas on the chalkboard during the discussion): You all have excellent ideas! Let's apply as many as possible to our next area of study: fractions. Now, where can we begin?

(A bevy of moving hands and arms fill the air and an enthusiastic interest electrifies the room.)

What are your testing practices? Large-scale standardized tests are largely out of your hands, but when it comes to the tests you plan and administer yourself, you may be open to some input from A+ Teachers throughout the country. If so, don't miss this chapter.

> This chapter will show how you can make testing *almost* enjoyable
> by:
>
> - testing productively,
> - using a variety of approaches,
> - drawing students into making as well as taking tests, and
> - eradicating many of those causes of panic.

MAKE SURE YOU ARE TESTING FOR THE RIGHT REASONS

When asked why they test, both groups of teachers in our survey gave high priority to noble testing objectives such as:

- to see if students understand concepts and processes being studied,
- to get an indication of student progress and achievement (for grading and planning purposes), and
- to evaluate teaching quality and procedures. ("Am I getting through?")

The practices of A+ Teachers do, however, differ from those of Other Teachers in some very significant ways. They give fewer tests in general, and they . . .

Avoid using tests to motivate student learning

"Motivational" tests purporting to intensify student effort are generally believed to be incentives, especially for lazy, sluggish, uncooperative, or disinterested students. Unfortunately, such tests are often counter-productive and create resentment, dislike of subject and teacher, absenteeism, or all of the above!

As one A+ Teacher put it: "Learning must be for self-satisfaction, not to pass a test!" The most dedicated teachers do indeed find a host of more creative, more exciting, and more effective ways to encourage students to put forth their best efforts. Such as? Re-read the previous twelve chapters for examples galore!

Give fewer tests to reinforce student test-taking skills

Granted, we live in a "test-taking" world, where licenses, degrees, and jobs often demand knowledge of how to prepare for, and take, some form of test. Most survey participants at one time or another have tested for the purpose of improving student skills in test-taking, but A+ Teachers are far less likely to do so. These teachers are more interested in the joy of learning than in the anatomy of test-passing!

Use diagnostic tests moderately

Tests which are "stepping stones" to learning are looked upon favorably by outstanding teachers. They use them moderately, whereas Other Teachers tend to overlook or to rely too heavily on them.

Herman L. Forbes tests once in a while to locate individual *strengths and weaknesses* so he can plan appropriate learning activities; Hazel C. Morton considers test results when she prepares materials and gives *individual or group lessons*; and Edward E. Bowman uses pre-tests to determine students' *expectancy levels*, which become "starting points" for working individually with his junior high school students.

Such tests are effective as *indicators*—not dictators. For forming instructional groups and making plans, diagnostic tests can be helpful, but A+ Teachers apparently rely on equally important clues, like their own observations of the students or the needs evidenced day by day in the classroom setting.

TAMPER WITH TRADITION—FIND SOME PRODUCTIVE ALTERNATIVES!

Teachers' contracts do not specify that tests must always be of the all too common sit-down, no-peeking, pencil-and-paper variety—generally characterized by high pressure and the widespread urge to cheat. So why not zero in on student achievements and needs in some novel ways, giving both yourself and your students a "lift" in the process? You may, for example:

Try different types of pencil-and-paper tests

In a college study that I conducted, 60 students were asked what test form they most, and least, preferred. Multiple-choice structure rated high, probably because it helps to rekindle known but forgotten answers. True-false and fill-in types, however, were among the most disliked, the former due to their ambiguity and the latter mostly due to their stress on picayune facts. *Essay tests* were high on both lists—preferred by some because they allow more than a surface, or factual, display of knowledge, and disliked by others because of the subjective evaluations they sometimes elicit from teachers.[1]

How right these students are! In one experiment an essay test paper received scores ranging from 50-98% when graded by a number of competent teachers. To lessen this problem, essay tests can be structured more objectively. For example, rather than just asking students to compare the Greeks and Romans, you may give them a more specific essay assignment, which can be more uniformly evaluated, such as:

> Compare the Greeks and Romans in the following areas. Give a minimum of two examples for each:
>
> A. Food and dress,
>
> B. Religious beliefs,
>
> C. Cultural contributions.[2]

Supplement tests with more appealing means of evaluation.

Competent teachers often rely rather heavily on their *own observations*. Gil Marshall administers very few paper-and-pencil tests, depending instead on careful daily observations. Diane Liskow cites observation as the main alternative to testing. She believes that a teacher who knows the students, is sensitive to their feelings and needs, and aware of their accomplishments, can in many ways evaluate progress far better than a test.

Oral testing is another technique which some teachers find preferable to the traditional test, especially for students who are deficient in reading and writing skills. It also rules out bluffing, copying, and other hazards inherent in written evaluations; and—particularly if coupled with careful monitoring of gestures and facial expressions to minimize misunderstandings—its accuracy can be high.

Maxel J. Ferguson considers verbal testing to be not only more accurate, but also less threatening to his elementary students, most of whom are in the process of learning English. Helen B. Guptill and Wally Bain favor the same approach to guide their upper-grade students through individualized Science programs.

Other slants and alternatives which outstanding teachers have found effective include:

- *Open-book tests* during which students may fill gaps in their knowledge by consulting reference works. This teaches them *how* to learn, a skill which will be useful their entire lives (Mary C. Holden).

- *Informal problem-solving situations* in which students are asked to perform practical tasks (collecting milk money, making a holiday budget, writing to a sick friend, using an encyclopedia) to provide the teacher with evaluative data (Carol DeLorenzo).

- *Special class meetings* during which the teacher listens to student comments on, and individual interpretations of, completed studies—and gets a good idea of individual, group, and teacher accomplishments (Lois K. Smith).

- *Student projects* which uniquely reflect understanding and effort. For example, giving the class a general topic (such as the Jeffersonian era) and asking students to prepare themes on self-selected, related topics, or to react from a new viewpoint (such as a visiting Martian, Mr. Joe Citizen, Mary Minority). The resulting news articles, playlets, political cartoons, and even songs, jingles, and intricate poems, are exciting bases for evaluation (Vincent J. Vespe).

Try testing through games

A good way to take the "edge" off testing is to make it enjoyable so that the full extent of students' knowledge can surface.

Ruth Campopiano, who teaches high school Spanish, uses *crossword puzzles,* word games, riddles, and incomplete stories, legends, or fables to test knowledge and skills; E. Dean Makie uses *group games* with his junior high school students, often pitting team against team; and Mary C. Holden makes it fun to investigate topics of study by first recording what students believe they know about the subject, then challenging them to learn more. (Students later enjoy reviewing their previous "*misconceptions*," which are sometimes used as humorous true-false test items.)

Jean D'Arcy Maculaitis devised tests for foreign-born students that are both enjoyable and revealing. At elementary levels a *puppet* is the "administrator"; much of the testing is oral, in game-like form, with students responding to stories, flashcards, pictures, and the like. For upper-graders Ms. Maculaitis utilizes simple silent reading selections and fascinating *film tests* in which students interpret what they see and hear.[3]

Sharon A. Watson encourages her kindergarteners to test themselves through *game-like "activities,"* either singly or in pairs. Her students have fun with self-evaluative opportunities like these:

- *Measuring activity:* Different lengths of string are used to measure items in the room: table tops, aquarium, pencil, etc.
- *Collage activity:* Cards containing 2, 3, or 4 letters of the alphabet are selected, and items beginning with those letters are taken from the scrapbox and artistically arranged on a piece of paper.
- *Jewelry activity:* Necklaces and bracelets are made by copying shapes and patterns from task cards and gluing them onto a backing, as shown in Exhibit 13-1.

**EXHIBIT 13-1: SELF-TESTING JEWELRY MAKING
ACTIVITY (geometric shapes)**

Lita Grabeklis sometimes uses a *bingo-type format* (five rows of five empty boxes) to make testing more enjoyable. Students number their boxes as they please, and test questions are numbered, mixed up, and drawn from a container. Students write their answers in their appropriate boxes, and get their names on a "Bingo Awards Board" as they get five in a row—but all continue until the end of the test.

Rebecca Guess wants her primary students to have fun during their *listening quizzes*—and they do! They complete an appealing picture (such as the one in Exhibit 13-2) according to oral instructions given just once by Ms. Guess. This not only improves their listening ability and concentration, but it also gives them a chance to display their color awareness, left-right orientation, and arithmetic ability as they respond to directions like these:

1. With your black crayon, put a nose on the dog, and with your red crayon, color the boy's shirt red.
2. Put your name at the bottom right corner.

EXHIBIT 13-2: LISTENING QUIZ

3. Add two small windows to the dog's house.

4. The boy's house has three more windows than the dog's. Draw in the correct number of windows.

TURN TEST-TAKERS INTO TEST-MAKERS

One sure way of getting students to see tests in a new light is by giving them a part in their preparation. Helen Tieger's junior high school students often design *little quizzes* when they share small-group projects with the class. Ms. Tieger first tests the groups on their respective subjects (with her own tests); then the groups present their information to the class and administer their own original evaluations.

Carol Thollander encourages her fourth-graders to help prepare *large tests* by contributing test items or questions. She looks the entries over, discusses them with their contributors if necessary, and later incorporates as many as possible into her tests. She may also consult with the class in deciding which student-designed items should be included.

Dr. Glasser tells of a high school teacher who asks each student to submit *discussion questions* relevant to the study material as a standard weekly assignment. Questions are evaluated and returned to the students for revision, then used in examinations in which each student answers his or her *own* questions! Evaluations are based on the quality of both the questions *and* the answers.[4]

ALLEVIATE THOSE RESULT-DISTORTING TENSIONS

> I am sitting in a classroom. My hands shake with fright, and my heart races with relentless anxiety as the test is passed out . . . I hesitatingly turn the examination over to survey the questions . . . icy fear grips my entire being as my dread has actualized . . . I do *not* know the answers to *any* of the listed questions!

This is a recurring nightmare which often haunts me. I wonder how many of today's students will experience similar problems as the years go by. Not too many, if the A+ Teachers have anything to say about it!

Ever since Gunnar Horn noticed that "testing jitters" were having detrimental effects on his high school English students, he has been building *humorous "relief valves"* into his tests. These not only soothe the nerves so results are more reliable, but they also add some enjoyment to what are otherwise unpleasant experiences. He may, for example, "throw in" a few humorous multiple-choice items, such as:

Art Buchwald is:

    a) a disco champion
    b) a popular artist
    c) a German novelist
    d) principal of this high school

Archie Bunker's favorite propaganda device is:

    a) name calling
    b) card stacking
    c) bandwagon
    d) transfer trick

This test is:

    a) easy
    b) difficult
    c) mind-expanding
    d) weird

Or he may include true-false items guaranteed to draw chuckles from even the most "uptight" students:

T or F

Debbie advocates freedom of speech.

Bruce says chewing gum relaxes him; so we should all chew it.

Tim has had to fight off the girls since he switched to Hai Karate after-shave.

The test itself may end on a light note, with a task like this:

In *ten* words or less explain why this is the greatest course you ever took.

When students answer this final item, they no doubt frequently mention Mr. Horn's ability to put them at ease and make even testing fun![5]

"Super teachers" have devised countless ways to make tests less threatening so students can feel better—*and* do better. Here are a few good ideas and thoughtful accommodations:

Testing via the tape recorder. Individuals or small groups in Wally Bain's high school Science classes sometimes take tests in complete privacy with recorder and earphones. Answers are written down and corrected immediately by the student, a classmate, or the teacher.

Using different semantics. Donald DeVries has almost eliminated the word "test" from his vocabulary because of the paralyzing effect is has on his students. Instead, he refers to tests as evaluations, challenges, problems, or games, finding that these elicit more positive attitudes—and generally higher scores!

Making tests brief. Myrtle Collins makes sure that her tests cover only what she has taught and what students ought to know. She weeds out trifles and irrelevance so students are not overpowered by sheer volume or length and are more likely to do well.

Carolyn C. Haines and Rebecca Guess prefer frequent small tests to fewer large ones. Observes Ms. Haines: "Tests at close intervals minimize the threat and also encourage small successes." Ms. Guess gives simple, attractive tests (like the one in Exhibit 13-3) and schedules test-related conferences where students can explain and elaborate upon their answers.

Adopting a "no-grades-final" policy. Mario Fierros offers alternative tests (a variety of non-written evaluative activities) to

**EXHIBIT 13-3: A NON-THREATENING,
CONCISE TEST**

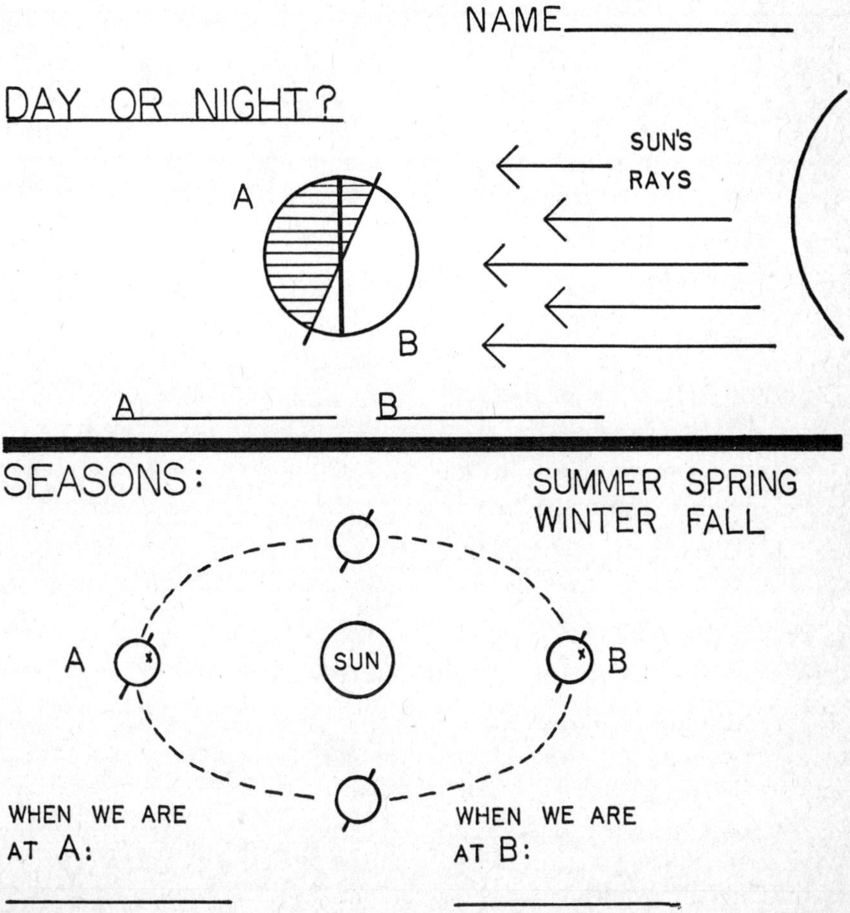

NAME_____

DAY OR NIGHT?

SUN'S RAYS

A

B

A _____ B _____

SEASONS: SUMMER SPRING
                            WINTER FALL

A   SUN   B

WHEN WE ARE   WHEN WE ARE
AT A: AT B:

_____   _____

his high school Spanish students who do poorly on the traditional tests.

Emily Ehm keeps her grade book in pencil and gives *all* of her junior high school students a chance to earn higher grades by submitting additional, improved work.

Carol Thollander's students can "up" their grades in much the same fashion, by handing in special reports within a week of the test or assignment.

Giving students leeway. In an educational experiment, a number of students were put into pairs to take an open-book test and were permitted to discuss their answers. Paired students did significantly better than students working alone; in fact, two "C" students often did better than an "A" student on his or her own. The students later opted for this type of testing because it lessened anxiety; it also increased their learning![6]

My husband, who was educated in Switzerland, tells of a high school teacher who would "slip" out of the classroom during testing sessions without forbidding his students to discuss the material or look up pertinent information. A curious student finally confronted the teacher about this unorthodox behavior, and got this explanation: "I *want* you to search for unknown answers, for by so doing you learn more—and that, after all, is what we are after!"

Perhaps the most important way in which a teacher can make testing a more positive and productive activity is by adhering to a few simple *guidelines:*

1. Consider that you have a variety of students. Use a variety of testing techniques.
2. Plan tests carefully with respect to purpose, clarity, and content. When in doubt, "test the test" on a colleague or other interested party.
3. Guide students in how and what to study.
4. Return tests as soon as possible and encourage students to discuss problem areas.
5. Give students more than a "mark."

It has been shown that just a few seconds' worth of extra thoughtfulness on the part of the teacher can make a world of difference in students' performance. Students awarded only a mark on their tests were least motivated, and received the lowest scores on the next test. Those given an impersonal but helpful comment in addition did noticeably better on the following test. And those who had the highest scores "next time around" were those whose teachers cared enough to add comments which were not only helpful but also personalized and thus particularly relevant to the individual students.[7]

*   *   *   *   *   *

Perhaps some day test-related nightmares will be nonexistent, and students can recall displaying their knowledge and skills as a pleasant experience. Meanwhile, we can seek a balance between preparing students for the rigors of testing which face them in life, testing to monitor progress, and testing to improve both teaching and learning.

We should, however, keep in mind a thought which permeates this entire book: that *concern for the students* is of utmost importance in achieving success as a teacher. This concern should be reflected even in the way tests are constructed, administered, graded, *and* used!

*   *   *   *   *   *

14 HOW TO RETAIN SANITY WHILE KEEPING TRACK OF STUDENT PROGRESS

Whether you must monitor the progress of two hundred students for one subject or twenty-five students in a dozen subjects, it is an awesome responsibility which can, at times, be frustrating.

Let's see what one elementary teacher has done to streamline record-keeping and to make it more beneficial to teacher and students alike. Here she explains her procedures to a group of interested parents during Parent Visitation Night:

Teacher: "What memories do you have of this little book?" (She holds up the commercially produced gradebook. Parents reluctantly tell of dreads, fears, resentments, and dishonesties, but also of healthy competition, a sense of responsibility, and the like.)

Teacher: "You will be glad to know that this little book will not hold the third-grade fate of your children, because it will not be the sole record of their performance. It is just one of many ways in which we will be monitoring progress this year—and some of them will actively involve your children ... and you!

"The students and I already use these weekly checklists (holding up a sample) to keep track of how each day is spent. And every Friday we have private conferences during which we compare our notes and jointly decide what area or areas may require special attention during the following week. We try to concentrate on just one or two things, such as more legible penmanship and better spelling, or whatever.

"This is where you parents enter the picture! Checklists and class-work are sent home each weekend. Please discuss them with your children. Don't do any work over the weekend—the weekend is for relaxation—but commend your children on work done well and on the positive comments you will always find in the folder. Then sit down with your children and plan ways in which you can concentrate on the "special attention" areas during the coming week.

"Students who demonstrate marked improvement or sincere effort in these special areas by the next conference will have the honor of displaying an example of their work on that large bulletin board in the back of the room entitled 'We Thought We Could . . . and We Proved It!'

"In addition, as you browse around the room tonight, you will see other ways in which students keep their own records: the independent testing graphs in our Math Center, the 'Books I've Read' listings in the large notebook in the Library Corner, the 'Special Projects' charts on the far wall, and the self-evaluation sheets available to students after any completed activity.

"And so, mothers and fathers, this little red book we all recall from our school experience will not be the 'end all' for *your* children. Their final marks will be based also on the weekly checklists, the charts, the listings, the graphs, our weekly conferences, and their day-to-day achievements. If you have any questions, please see me personally before you leave this evening. Thank you for coming . . . and thank you, in advance, for your help! Your interest and assistance will be a very valuable asset to your children!"

As you read this chapter, you will find that record-keeping can be vastly improved by:

- using achievement displays judiciously,
- setting up a simple but effective student folder or file system,
- working with versatile multi-purpose checklists,
- finding sophisticated supplements to the "little red book," and
- letting students lend a hand in monitoring their own progress.

USE ACHIEVEMENT DISPLAYS WISELY

A+ Teachers use progress displays—but with reservations! They are less likely than Other Teachers to never make a progress-related display, and even *less* likely to use them constantly. Are they more cautious because such open displays can be misused in ways which might hurt certain students?

First-grade teacher Lugarda Sandoval warns: "Displays of progress charts can be harmful. I use them only if I feel the group will be helped by it." Mrs. Virgil M. Linderoth, who teaches grade five, points out that displays are generally too embarrassing to low achievers; so she only uses this approach when no grades are indicated.

Despite these dangers, this record-keeping technique is well used—especially by elementary teachers and teachers with a good deal of classroom experience—as a way of "keeping track" and simultaneously encouraging learning. How, then, can it be made to work?

Charles Zeichner and other A+ Teachers use *display check-off sheets* which enable students to register their own progress by marking off completed tasks, knowledge gained, skills demonstrated, goals attained, and the like.

I have successfully used *bulletin board displays* featuring baseball "games," cartoon characters, and rockets heading for the moon. Students made small cut-outs and moved them along a prescribed path as progress was made. Such displays enhanced the joy of accomplishment and often inspired students to help one another by mutual testing and tutoring.

The best displays invariably invite a minimum of comparisons among students and a maximum of student self-awareness. One teacher achieved this blend by *having students make and display booklets* listing their individual projects, special assignments, test scores, etc.— with attractively designed covers!

Junior high school teacher Helen B. Guptill periodically shows *group progress charts,* in bar graph form, with an overhead projector in the dramatic setting of the school auditorium. On the big screen, students can see how their classes stand in relation to the others in terms of completed LAP's or study units. No individual progress charts are ever projected, but interested students often take their own personal record-keeping charts along to make private comparisons.

UTILIZE STUDENT FOLDERS EFFECTIVELY

Many A+ Teachers—especially elementary and inner-city teachers—prefer to use some type of folder or file system as a record-keeping aid.

Cook, Caldwell, Christiansen, and the other contributors to the book entitled "The Come-Alive Classroom" suggest keeping student files containing the following materials for use at conferences or to facilitate individual performance appraisals:

- progress sheets, charts, etc.
- notes and observations of the teacher,
- important, or representative, daily papers, and
- test papers.

They also recommend that teachers prepare and duplicate *forms* for speed and efficiency—such as oral reading skills checklists, charts for noting quiz and test scores, personal qualities listings, and whatever other records may be useful. Such files may, or may not, be made accessible to students, depending upon the purposes and nature of the data.[1]

Don Gibson's junior high school Mathematics students keep their own folders, similar to the ones their teacher keeps, so they always know where they "stand." In Sarah Schreiner's class, too, a *dual set of folders* is maintained, but for different purposes. One set is available to students and contains work to be done: workbooks, books to read, and special assignments. The second set—with long-range records such as test scores, sample papers, and day-to-day observations—is used mainly for conferences with parents or students, and for teacher planning.

Each of Marie Hanlon's fifth-graders keeps his or her own *notebook and file.* While notebooks serve as the students' own progress-records, the files hold completed papers, tests, and other written work. These are reviewed weekly by Ms. Hanlon prior to being taken home for parent scrutiny. Parents may keep the contents and return the signed file so that it can be re-filled during the following week.

MAKE CHECKLISTS TO IDENTIFY STUDENT (AND TEACHER) STRENGTHS AND WEAKNESSES

Checklists are efficient tools for recording many things: homework returned, assignments completed, skills mastered, and so on—and A+ Teachers use them much more than Other Teachers.

Therese Anglin reproduces a *class list* with rows of empty boxes following the names. By adding headings such as "Private Conferences Completed," "Visits to Science Center," "Test Scores," or whatever is needed, she has checklists galore at her fingertips!

Kathryn A. Gillespie gives her students *checklists of objectives* to be met. A checklist for the study of Alaska may include the following:

_____ 1. Locate Alaska on a map or globe.

_____ 2. Name important cities and resources.

_____ 3. Read a pertinent book.

_____ 4. Do independent research on a chosen topic.

_____ 5. Write a story set in Alaska.

_____ 6. Select or create your own Alaska-related activity.

In line with management-by-exception principles, Alex Dobrowolski uses *minimum checklists* to keep track of forgotten books or pens, tardiness, incomplete or missing assignments, etc. Because these are dealing with the exceptions rather than with the rule, he finds them to be particularly "energy efficient."

At the opposite end of the spectrum are *"maxi checklists"* such as the one in Exhibit 14-1, which profile the entire year's progress of a student in Math. Extra columns can be added to record recurring errors, results of periodic re-checks, exceptional proficiencies, and so on.

Student-made checklists can add a new dimension in record-keeping, and they can be undertaken by the entire class together, small groups of students, or individuals. Contents can encompass just about anything: words one would like to learn to spell, questions to be resolved during a study unit, ways to attain a desired objective, resources to investigate, or items to study for a test.

To analyze our own effectiveness, we teachers may design and use *self-evaluation checklists* with soul-searching headings such as:

- *"Am I Varying My Teaching Methods?"* Listings could include multi-class meetings, entire class lessons, small-group endeavors, individualized approaches, student-directed activities, peer-teaching, etc., and they could be filled in weekly or by study topic.

- *"Have I Correlated All Subjects?"* This could entail a list of subjects (Math, Language, Spelling, Art, Reading, and so on) and vertical columns to record the study units.

- *"Am I Ignoring Anyone?"* It is easy to neglect certain students, generally the "average" or particularly reticent ones. A class list with column headings like "Talked with Child,"

EXHIBIT 14-1: YEARLY CHECKLIST FOR MATHEMATICS

Name of student: _____

Subject: Math

	Intro-duced	Needs Imp.	O.K.
1. Adding 1-dig. nos.	—	—	—
2. Subt. 1-dig. nos.	—	—	—
3. Adding 2-dig. nos. (no carrying)	—	—	—
4. Subt. 2-dig. nos. (no borrowing)	—	—	—
5. Adding 2-dig. nos. (with carrying)	—	—	—
6. Subt. 2-dig. nos. (with borrowing)	—	—	—
7. Etc.	—	—	—

"Assisted Child," "Reprimanded Child" and "Chose Child for Special Honor" reveals how teacher time is allotted.

GET AWAY FROM THAT "LITTLE RED BOOK"!

A significant difference between the two groups of teachers surveyed is that A+ Teachers use the commercial gradebook far less often than Others. They "branch out" to include a wealth of effective evaluative techniques. They may, for example:

Chart student progress

Carolyn C. Haines' students decorate attractive *book charts* like the one in Exhibit 14-2 for keeping track of books which have

EXHIBIT 14-2: BOOK CHART

#	TITLE	DATE
1.		
2.		
3.		
4.		
5.		
6.		

BOOKS I'VE READ
(NAME)

been read and discussed with their teacher. During special study units, Jane Brake's high school students complete activity *score-sheets,* as shown in Exhibit 14-3, which relieve their teacher of excessive record-keeping, enable them to "keep an eye on themselves," and assure them of a balanced "mix" of independently selected experiences.

Helen B. Guptill and Don Gibson use *overall progress charts* (Exhibits 14-4 and 14-5) to monitor the accomplishments of their many junior high school students. Ms. Guptill lists each topic of study in her Science curriculum, and Mr. Gibson arranges his chart by Mathematics units (A = adding, S =subtraction, etc.), noting results of diagnostic tests (D), progress check-ups (P), and unit evaluations.

Use index-card wizardry

Diane Mazzei always has 3x5-inch cards at hand for *on-the-spot notes* about her primary students, including their achievements ("successfully sounded words using left-to-right scanning technique") and problems ("reversed saw and was.") In Mathematics and Reading, Josephine Brown uses *skill cards* representing single skills. Individual student names are added as the particular skills are mastered.

Charles Y. Hoyt keeps *student information cards* for easy access to test grades and anecdotal observations; Opal B. Melvin has *project cards* on which her high school students record descriptions of completed projects; and Wally Bain uses *inventory flip charts* (charts reproduced onto file cards and kept in commercially produced flip-

	READING	LISTENING		VIEWING		SPEAKING
	Books – Short Selections	Records	Speakers	Films	TV	Oral Reports
WEEK I						
WEEK II						
WEEK III						
WEEK IV						
WEEK V						

EXHIBIT 14-3: ACTIVITY SCORESHEET

chart containers) for noting marks, homework status, specific achievements, and problem areas.

EXHIBIT 14-4: PROGRESS CHART

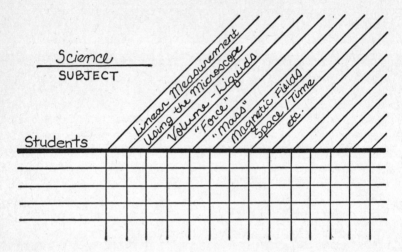

Cy Sommer devised a unique system using *data cards*, like the one in Exhibit 14-6, which were printed at the school's vocational shop. These are filled in by his students after each Baking session. He reviews them and puts them into a permanent record-keeping file.

Put it between covers

Chris Sabo uses a *three-ring looseleaf* binder as a "class book" for recording all progress data in chart form, and my third-graders and I transformed such a binder into an original collection of "third-grade autobiographies." Each student had his or her own section in the book for entering grades, notes concerning strengths and weaknesses, and sample papers. This book was far more than just my "class log"; it inspired students and pleased parents with its indisputable evidence of the noteworthy progress being made.

Helen A. Thomas delights in updating her *"good news booklet."* Each time she notices something commendable about a student, she jots it down on his or her page in the booklet. At report card time, she has an abundance of material to draw from, and she can always write a paragraph of happy, encouraging information which might otherwise have been forgotten.[2]

EXHIBIT 14-5: INDIVIDUALIZED MATHEMATICS CHART

STUDENTS PERIOD 1	Unit 1	Unit 2	Unit 3 A	Unit 3 A	Unit 3 S	Unit 3 S	Grade	Unit 4 M	Unit 4 M	Unit 4 D	Unit 4 D	Grade	Unit G 5	Unit G 6	Unit 7 F	Unit 7 F	Unit 7 A	Unit 7 A
	1	2	D1	P1	D2	P2	Grade	D3	P3	D4	P4	Grade	5	6	D5	P5	D6	P6
Adams, May																		
Anderson, Joe																		
Brown, Carrie																		

173

EXHIBIT 14-6: RECORD-KEEPING CARD (3 x 5 inches)

Name		Date	Production Unit	
Quantity Ordered	Quantity Made	Product	Time Started	Time Finished

Sanitation Assignment: Time lost:

Try a system with "punch"

In conjunction with a special independent reading program, primary teacher Rebecca Guess devised *punch-out cards* with numbers representing stories to be read (Exhibit 14-7.). After reading a story, the student answers questions about it, discusses answers with the teacher, and gets to punch out the corresponding number on the card. When all fifteen are punched out, the card is filed, and the child receives a new card representing fifteen slightly more difficult stories.

EXHIBIT 14-7: PUNCH-OUT READING CARD

"The children love the hole punching," reports Ms. Guess, "and they learn filing techniques because cards, stories, and question sheets must be located and returned daily." Moreover, the improvement she has noted in reading skills since the onset of her program has been phenomenal!

Punch-out unit sheets, made from duplicated blank forms with punched out holes (Exhibit 14-8), not only are time savers for teachers but also are enjoyed by students. As job requirements are fulfilled, the sections between the appropriate hole and the edge are removed with a horseshoe-shaped paper punch. Thus, when the sheets are collected and stacked, one can instantaneously determine who

EXHIBIT 14-8: PUNCH-OUT UNIT SHEET

Art Project	Test	Small Group Activity	Oral Presentation of Facts
Music Project	STUDY OF *Colonial Times*		4 Selected homework papers
Creating Math Problems	NAME *Jane Doe*		Learning Center Activities
Free Choice book read	Research paper	Special spelling words	Booklet (prepared)

has not completed a certain activity by pushing a pencil through that particular hole to see which papers remain on the "skewer."

INCREASE MOTIVATION BY GIVING STUDENTS A MORE ACTIVE ROLE IN RECORD–KEEPING

To get students more involved, Kent Schipper presents them with challenges! He may, for example, set a goal of *1,000 points* for nine week's work, and let students earn them through classwork, extra credit assignments, and study-related projects. Records are naturally being kept by the students, who take pride in seeing their scores go up and up.

Carol Thollander has her students bring home original *monthly report cards* to motivate them to discuss their progress with their families; achievements of Jean D'Arcy Maculaitis' students are the subject of *"parental postcards"* which are written in the native languages of her foreign-born pupils and mailed to their homes; and Michael Mason's Physical Education students are thrilled to be "bearers of glad tidings" by carrying home *spontaneous notes,* like the one in Exhibit 14-9, describing class activities and individual accomplishments.

EXHIBIT 14-9: NOTE CORRESPONDENCE TO PARENTS

> May 2
>
> This week in physical education class we are playing floor hockey. John scored two goals in the game today. Ask him about them.
>
> Mike Mason

Other A+ Teachers have found that the more monitoring responsibilities students shoulder the more motivated they become—due to the constant feedback. And so . . .

- Kindergarteners describe, date, and illustrate their learning (skipping, writing their names, counting, etc.) in individual *"brag books,"* which become treasured collections of memories for their families (Sharon A. Watson).

- Primary students check off completed assignments on their own individual *contract* forms (Winnefred M. Haugland).

- Third-graders dramatize their progress during a 10-day series of timed multiplication tests by keeping their own *improvement graphs* as in Exhibit 14-10 (Ruth A. Tschudin).

EXHIBIT 14-10: PROGRESS GRAPH

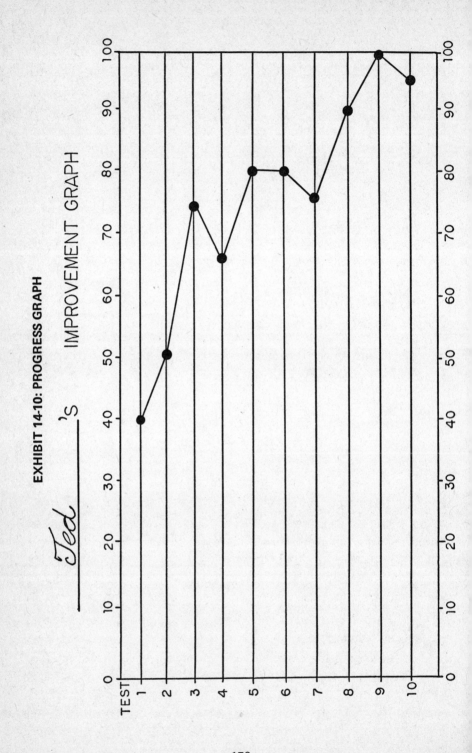

Ted 's   IMPROVEMENT GRAPH

- Junior high school Remedial Reading students fill in *planning/record-keeping schedules* with goals and activities for the coming three weeks. Performance is reviewed frequently during private conferences (Barbara Webster).

- High school students periodically write their own *personal progress reports* for their parents, and they include brief study outlines, work samples, and self-appraisals of their progress. Parents are delighted, and students are encouraged to "keep up the good work!" (New Jersey teacher).

* * * * * *

To avoid being bogged down by the drudgery of record-keeping, A+ Teachers do all they can to make it manageable. Simultaneously, they endeavor to make it more meaningful—for themselves, their students, and parents, too!

Their secret "recipe" is variety, creativity, and student involvement. With a sprinkling of checklists, folders, charts, and original record-keeping aids, they "cook up a storm" that gets the job done efficiently and to the satisfaction of all involved.

* * * * * *

15 HOW TO BLEND KEY "SUCCESS CHARACTERISTICS" WITH YOUR TEACHING SKILLS

What personal characteristics and outside interests set A+ Teachers apart from Other Teachers? Here are two youngsters who have noticed some interesting facts about the teacher they hope to get. Let's listen in on their conversation:

Pete: Who do you want for your teacher next year?

Pat: Mrs. Williams. I sure hope I get her!

Pete: Me, too! I think everybody wants her. She's really "neat."

Pat: Yeah. Her students get to laugh a lot—and they do exciting things.

Pete: But you'll work hard if you get her. She really makes you learn!

Pat: I know—and I don't mind. She works hard, too, and yet *she's* always smiling, so I guess I'll be like that when I'm in her class.

Pete: She sure is smart! She's president of the teachers' group, you know.

Pat: She was also my brother's Sunday School teacher!

Pete: And she does volunteer work at the hospital. I know because my mom saw her there last week.

Pat: What I like best about her is that she's nice to everyone— *especially* kids!

Pete: And as a teacher, she's tops!

Pat: That's right. She really tries harder than the others—and I'm going to *hope* harder than anyone that I get her next year!

This concluding chapter will tell you about the personalities of A+ Teachers, and how:

- humor and enthusiasm can be educational "plusses,"
- our own past has lessons to teach us,
- good student rapport can make a huge difference,
- effort and hard work are essential to effective teaching, and
- we all have something to learn from our colleagues' successes.

LET HUMOR AND ENTHUSIASM WORK FOR YOU!

A+ Teachers are patient, understanding, consistent, and well-organized, as are most of their conscientious but less successful colleagues. But there are two personality traits—humor and enthusiasm—which are put to significantly greater classroom use by the most effective teachers. So . . .

Bring a smile or laugh to your students

- Margaret J. Payne feels that patience and keeping a *sense of humor* at all times have helped to make her an effective teacher.
- Mrs. Jett Campbell is guided by a three-part "formula": (1) love of students, (2) enjoyment of work involved, and (3) well-developed sense of humor.
  Lily DeCleir opts for another threesome: (1) hard work, (2) fairness, and (3) *laughter.*
- Jerry L. Craven credits his success to high standards, consistency, helpfulness, and *strictness tempered by humor.*
- Connie Anderson feels that being a *"character"* has made her a better teacher.

Humor may not be paramount in the outstanding educational achievements of these and other A+ Teachers, but research substantiates the difference it can make. A study of three inner-city junior high schools showed that the teachers with the most eager, interested students were those who: oriented them to subject matter, explained expectations and standards, took no nonsense (yet spent almost no time in a drill sergeant's role), dealt carefully with student feelings, spent more time praising than criticizing, *smiled often, and joked a good deal.* [1]

The University of Southern California did a 2½-year study of comedy in the classroom. TV comedy writer Eric Cohen spiced up teachers' lecture notes with humor—without changing content. Students given the *added touch of humor* scored higher in both comprehension and retention of the material than those receiving the conventional lectures! [2]

Illinois Language Arts teacher Emily Ehm often prefaces activities with comments like: "Isn't school getting dull? Aren't you bored? Wouldn't it be funny if . . . ?" "Wouldn't you enjoy . . . ?" Initiated by such a *lighthearted approach* was a launching of balloons with the message "This is an experiment to see how far love will go!" The responses students received from people in Ohio, West Virginia, and Virginia sparked many enthusiastic correspondences.

To Gunnar Horn, a good hearty laugh serves as a "pacifier." It clears the air and is contagious. He is not a joke-teller, but he uses *humorous anecdotes and good-natured teasing.* He keeps clear of comments like "Where were you brought up, in a barn?", which may hurt, but he may say: "That's a beautiful answer—I wish it was right!" or "Don't be in too big a hurry to answer, Jim. Remember, whatever you say may be used against you!"

The best laughing experiences, he finds, grow out of *subject matter.* When a student writes an unclear sentence (such as: "The exchange student told about mosquitoes in Mr. Davey's Sociology class in his native Ghana.") Mr. Horn may, rather than criticizing, simply react with a comment like: "Do you really mean that?" "You could be sued for libel!" "Please repeat that!" "Will you run it by again?" or "Let's have an instant re-play!" This generally makes the student aware that there is an error—and often results in a chorus of student requests to hear the sentence so they can all laugh amiably together. [3]

Display the enthusiasm you'd like to see in your students

"Enthusiasm makes the difference!" says Norman Vincent Peale[4]—and it has certainly made a big difference for John M. Selig, Robert Glover, and countless other A+ Teachers.

- June Betsworth's *enthusiasm for journalism* inspired her to start a club called PEN (People in Elementary Newspapers) for teachers from all parts of the U.S. who work with classroom or school newspapers. Members exchange ideas and information through the club newsletter and much student excitement is generated through competitions and special events.[5]

- Because of her *enthusiasm for reading,* Audrey Stanton shares good literature with her elementary students daily— with such feeling that they "live" the story with her! Her enthusiasm is so contagious that a student who hated school and would not even read a paragraph unless forced to do so now can't be pried away from books and wants to continue his education. A partner teacher who left the school system was so affected by Ms. Stanton's enthusiasm that she made a plaque for her saying "To the best teacher *I* ever had!"

Top-rated teachers have a greater *enthusiasm for teaching* than their more average colleagues. They spend more of their own money for school-related materials, and more of their own time on school-related work. They give more of themselves to voluntary school activities and educational endeavors. For example:

- Helen B. Guptill is available for *half an hour daily before school.* Students know that if they have special needs, wish to catch up on missed assignments, or just want to talk this time is theirs!

- Moke C. Owens has *Saturday sessions* for the enjoyment and enrichment of interested students in his junior high school Music and Humanities classes.

- Lois K. Smith often does hall bulletin boards and heads *all-school campaigns* with themes like "Let's Stop Pollution." She also writes and produces an annual play for the PTA.

- Music teacher Fred Miller, Jr., gives his assistance to the Project Head Start program in his school, uses his *unscheduled time* to visit classrooms where he is not assigned that week, and spends the first fifteen minutes of each school day with guitar in hand serenading the primary classes to get them off to a good start!

- Billy J. Pack works on a legislative committee and has been *president,* treasurer, and parliamentarian of his district's teachers association.

Such is the enthusiasm of A+ Teachers—not just the "bubbly" type, but an excitement "from within"—that even when more lucrative opportunities arise, they may *prefer to remain in the "teacher's seat."* Connie Anderson refused three offers for school principalship; Harry H. Koch left his administrative position to return to his high school teaching post; and Edward Helwick, Jr., gave up his career as a writer for radio and TV shows to teach in a California high school—a decision he has never regretted.

Also apparent is the A+ Teachers' *enthusiasm for professional and personal growth.* They are often found doing something exciting and uplifting. For example:

- Edward Helwick spent summers studying at the Universities of Paris and Geneva. He taught a year in a Danish high school on a *Fulbright Grant,* and supervised 180 American students in Rome, Paris, Geneva, and London.

- Norene Perisi pursued and won *Instructor's "Dream Dollar Award"* to create Science kits; Harold Cotler received a *mini-grant* for his students to prepare audio-visual materials; Elsie F. Hart used a *Phi Delta Kappa grant* to establish an after-school program designed to counteract school failure; and Rinna Wolfe acquired a *fellowship* to teach 1,000 children their legal rights with a course on "Children and the Law."

- At least 20% of the A+ Teachers surveyed wrote *magazine articles,* had ideas published in educational periodicals, or pursued activities which made the news!

- A number are writing *books,* and a few already have! Harold Cotler's task card set, "NJ 4.U.2.C." (DPR Publishers, Inc.) and his *Encyclopedic Deskbook of Teaching Ideas and Classroom Activities* (Parker Publishing Company, Inc.) are already on the market, as is Essie Kirkland Hendley's *So You Want To Be a Teacher* (Carlton Press). Jean D'Arcy Maculaitis' book, *Essentials of English As a Second Language (ESL) Measurement and Evaluation,* will soon be available.

APPLY YOUR PAST TO THE "HERE AND NOW"!

Yes, A+ Teachers draw all they can from their past; our survey reveals that they get more mileage from their *college training,* finding it to be an important factor in their day-to-day success. This is substantiated by the findings of the Coleman Commission that the only characteristic of a school correlating with the achievement of its students is the intellectual attainment of the teachers. [6]

Carl R. Berg commends outstanding college professors for molding his educational "philosophies," shaping his teaching methods, and even helping him through his first year in the classroom. Donovan J. Holderness credits a particular college professor for being a great inspiration: "His personality was extraordinary; he took a definite interest in me; and he could present a topic in such a way that you couldn't help but learn it."

Even the "School of Hard Knocks" can be an invaluable teaching asset. Margaret D. Fleming, for example, considers the years she spent in the business world to be the major reason for her ability to give her Business Education students the realistic and thorough preparation they want and need. Others cite what many might consider to be negative factors:

- During Lynn Lothian's student teaching experience, her cooperating teacher had educational methods *differing radically* from hers. A horrible experience? On the contrary— it was the greatest incentive she ever had to pursue her own goals and ideals!

- As a teaching intern, Cy Sommer was told to *stop bringing in new ideas* or he would "burn himself out." Did this dampen his enthusiasm? It only challenged him to prove the opposite—that a person burns himself out when he *stops* growing!

- One teacher feels that her own personal *problems* have made her a more sensitive teacher, able to see more clearly what truly matters in life. Another person teaches from a wheelchair and maintains that what appears to be a drawback has been a positive success factor. Her students are generally more attentive and respectful because of the personal victory the wheelchair symbolizes!

DEVELOP A HEALTHY RAPPORT WITH STUDENTS

A+ Teachers cited a *close, understanding relationship* with their students as an important success factor more often than Other Teachers. Jean D'Arcy Maculaitis has engendered such a rapport;

suspended students sneak into the school through a back stair-case—just to attend *her* class!

Kindergarten teacher James A. Harris strives to develop it with his very young students right from the start by visiting each child prior to the beginning of the school year. Thus, that first day of school becomes a happy "re-acquaintance" time rather than a frightening experience for his students![7]

To Gunnar Horn, rapport is a *two-way street*. He attributes much of his success to the interest his high school students have taken in him! In a humorous newspaper article, he writes that what he has taught his students remains questionable, but that Bob taught him to ride horses, Malcomb got him interested in flying, Chuck instructed him in the art of paddling a canoe, Doug trained him in the use of a slide rule, Mark lectured him on how to shovel snow without breaking his back, and Gene showed him how to operate a tape recorder.[8]

How can a teacher develop good rapport with students? Here are just a few approaches to consider:

1 *Listening.* Edward E. Bowman is receptive to student complaints, needs, and interests—and responds with appropriate solutions, concern, and encouragement. Winnefred M. Haugland "tunes in" to constructive criticism from other teachers, administrators, parents, *and* students. But she also listens to her own feelings in order to be at ease with herself.

2. *Caring.* Dorothy A. Jacob takes a sincere interest in her students, and lets them know that she wants each to succeed in life. Barbara Payne tries to treat students as if they were her own children, frequently asking herself, "What would I do if this were *my* child?" Another teacher even asks: "How would I feel if *I* were this child?"

3. *Watching your attitudes.* Margaret J. Payne maintains that no child is ever a failure and wants her students to feel the same way about themselves. Lily DeCleir "saw" a child who had been left back not as a failure but as a highly respected, mature, success-ful student—which is exactly what he became! Rinna Wolfe's "never give up on anyone" attitude has changed many a student's life. She keeps this little story in mind to help her aim for each child's "balance springs":

> A bar of iron has small value, yet if it is made into knives its value increases. If it is used for needles its value goes up again. And if con-verted into balance springs for watches its value soars!

4. *Acting your ideals.* Ernest Rondeau cares about his high school Spanish students and shows it by his participative teaching methods and his accessibility. In Lily DeCleir's class love and concern are a "permanent part of the teaching agenda," as illustrated by an incident with a student who was about to pass out party invitations to all but one girl. Ms. DeCleir investigated and found that the girl with crutches was not invited for fear that she could not join in the games. After a talk with the parents and discussion of a parallel story with the class, the problem was solved to the benefit of all.

According to our survey, A+ Teachers act their ideals *outside of school,* too. They are more involved in civic affairs, service organizations, and religious activities. Charleen Hickey belongs to a community foreign-language organization; Doris Harder works as a volunteer probation counselor for young people; Katherine H. Kearney writes articles for church periodicals; Barbara E. Carlson works on a committee planning summer camps for retarded children; and Maralene Wesner, a minister's wife *and* Oklahoma Teacher of the Year, has done the following and more:

- organized a summer day camp program,
- taught Sunday School and held offices as Youth and Church Training Director,
- been organist, pianist, and leader of the children's church choir,
- developed a music training course for small churches,
- edited the *Braille Evangel,* an inspirational magazine for the blind,
- attended the Baptist World Congress in Japan, and played piano for a goodwill tour in Egypt,
- led tours to Europe, the Middle and Far East, preparing slide and motion picture travelogs for church, community, and school use.

BE PREPARED TO PAY THE PRICE!

Good teaching requires discipline, dedication, and maybe even sacrifice—all of which enhance both the goal *and* the seeker. Survey results show that sincere effort and hard work are success factors which separate great teachers from others in the field.

Thomas Alva Edison said he owed his success to 99% perspiration and just 1% inspiration; and so it is with teaching. Much that is seen as talent and giftedness is largely plain old effort and hard work. The *"teacher success formula,"* based on the hundreds of teachers in our survey, is this:

Be willing to work hard

A+ Teachers are generally found counting the benefits—not the cost. Lily DeCleir *staggers reading groups* to give her second-graders the quality and quantity of reading instruction they need and deserve. Two reading groups arrive an hour early, and the other two stay an hour later. A longer teaching day? Yes, but Ms. DeCleir willingly pays the price!

A+ Teachers are found working on the school *yearbook* (Emily Ehm) or an award-winning school *newspaper* (Edward Helwick); voluntarily conducting the high school *chorus* (Alice Purdes); organizing a bee keeping club or an all-school chess tournament (Richard H. Barber); creating *special classes* for exceptional students (Sheryl Hinman); teaching a *computer class* before school hours (John Selig); or even showing interested students how to play *tennis* (Donovan J. Holderness).

Gloryl Parchert is *audio-visual representative* for her school building, which entails storing and keeping track of equipment and files and overseeing their use; Jean D'Arcy Maculaitis organized a *"Mini Language Bank"* to better utilize the language talents of the teachers in her school district; Harry H. Koch, wanting a course to show his high school Science students the interaction between the different sciences, devised a *Science Literacy Course;* Rinna Wolfe implemented a variety of *Minority Studies* in her elementary school; and Emily Pritchard Carey produced a variety of original learning *kits* to make learning more exciting and enjoyable for her students. Is it worth the work? *All* emphatically answer "YES!!"

Get the students to work hard too!

A certain amount of *healthy stress* may be necessary if children are to learn. Work with 54 South Carolina elementary schools showed that students do best with a low-to-moderate amount of teacher criticism. This does not mean sarcasm, hostility, or personal criticism, but correcting deficient work and showing students how to improve.[9]

Should teachers take greater interest in their students' academic performance, or should they take greater interest in them personally? Thanks to Robert J. Blake and Jane Srygley Mouton, much of the business world knows that these two objectives are not mutually exclusive. The greatest success goes to those with a high interest in both people *and* performance.[10] Our survey confirmed this for teaching: A+ Teachers put great stress on rapport and student self-image, but they also devote themselves to *excellence* in education!

Higher academic standards and more concern for students require greater effort but also make teaching more challenging and rewarding. Here are some examples:

- In Mary Ann Brady's junior high school classes students receive *two grades* for each written assignment or test paper. The higher one applies if spelling is corrected and the paper re-submitted. This system evidences the great value she places on students as individuals, as well as on their academic performance.

- Janet L. Ryan combines high academic standards with personal warmth by expressing almost everything in *positive terms.* Comments like "Always walk" (rather than "Don't run"), "Papers I can read easily are a joy," and explanations about why certain things are learned or required are indicative of her concern for both the students and their accomplishments. This takes time and patience but pays off with gratifying results in student work and self-image.

- Clara Humphrey uses a *five-point system* to promote confidence and quality work in a group of low-ability high school English students. She awards one point for completed work, one for being prepared with a book, one for having pencil and paper, one for sincere effort, and one for high quality work. This entails more record-keeping for Ms. Humphrey, but has helped students to meet requirements and to gain satisfaction from exerting their best efforts.

My principal, Dominic Grassano, often helps teachers to reflect a bit and strive toward this ideal of *high standards combined with personal caring* by putting items of relevance into teacher mailboxes. Exhibit 15-1 is a sample of a note we received one day, and one which I always keep close at hand.

Caring for the students while motivating them toward fulfillment of their intellectual potential is the winning combination! Says Ralph Caputo: "We at Eugene Fields School are working for the children. *They* come first." Norma Munson sums it up this way:

EXHIBIT 15-1: NOTE FROM THE PRINCIPAL

BROADWAY SCHOOL

DO YOU KNOW . . .
- That the funny-nosed boy in the third row might become the doctor who saves your life?
- That the scientists working to protect your future once sat in a classroom at the grade level which you teach?
- That besides mother and father, you are the most important person in the world to most children?
- That lifelong scars are caused by a single statement made by teachers?
- That almost every "off the cuff" remark that you make is retold over the supper table?
- That children respect a tough teacher more than a pushover?
- That many children want to be just like you?

DO YOU . . .
- Really like children?
- Ever call a child "dumb"?
- Ever hate Monday?
- Ever transfer that feeling to your students?
- Ever pay as much attention to the girl with ragged shoes as to the one with new patent leather shoes?
- Ever come to school unprepared?
- Ever get angry when your students do the same?
- Ever rebel at that "extra" that's asked of you?
- Really like teaching?

WILL YOU . . .
- Continue to read and bring yourself up to date in the field of education?
- Strengthen yourself by taking college courses?
- Stand by and support your fellow teachers in all of their school endeavors?
- Support your PTA, although most parents don't?
- Take a sincere interest in every student who enters your classroom?

(Author Unknown)

"I expect a lot of my students. They know it, and I generally get what I expect. I enjoy helping them realize that they have more ability than they have ever used." What better gift can a teacher give a student?!

LEARN FROM SUPER TEACHER SUCCESSES

A national survey of parents of school-age children posed this question: "What is good about your child's school?" The answer most frequently received was "The teachers."[11]

We have been taking a close look at some dedicated and exceptional teachers—teachers like E. Dean Makie, who says, "I love to teach. I can't imagine myself doing anything else . . ."; teachers like Ann Koprowicz, who earnestly proclaims, "I love it!"; and teachers like Wally Bain, who feels this way: "I am what I am when I'm doing what I do; teaching is not my job, it is my *joy!*"

Each chapter of this book has laid out important lessons to be gleaned from outstanding teachers like these. We have learned a great deal about what they are doing and why they are so successful. The following thoughts and opinions, expressed by highly acclaimed teachers in our survey, give us additional points to ponder:

> Regardless of training, degrees, materials, machines, methods, etc., teaching in this country will never be any better than its individual teachers . . . .
>
> Unless teachers can remember that students and learning (and often parents and administrators) come before the "me" in teaching—unless they somehow regain some of that selfless dedication many of our predecessors prided themselves on—education and the priceless products of it can only suffer. Example is still the best teacher.
>
> Margaret Mecca
> Wyoming Teacher of the Year

> There is no single best method of teaching . . . . No materials are as yet "panaceas" to learning, and nothing "turns on" all students. The teacher is still the key. If a teacher is knowledgeable in an area, can communicate well with students, is enthusiastic, believes what is taught, and works hard with genuine devotion, is honest, fair, and objective in analyzing issues and lessons, then good quality learning should be achieved.
>
> William F. Higdon
> Missouri Teacher of the Year

What our country hopes to be starts in the classroom.

Edward Helwick, Jr.
California Teacher of the Year

And we, as individual teachers, can "start the ball rolling" right in our *own* classrooms! We'll take from the A+ Teachers whatever we can productively apply to our own unique situations—and use it to change lives for the better . . . our own included!

NOTES

HOW THIS BOOK CAN HELP YOU BECOME A MORE EFFECTIVE TEACHER

(1) The Teacher of the Year Program, sponsored annually by the Council of Chief State School Officers, *Encyclopedia Britannica,* and the *Ladies Home Journal,* singles out educators who inspire love of learning in students of all backgrounds and abilities.

CHAPTER ONE

(1) A book such as *1,001 Valuable Things You Can Get Free,* by Mort Weisinger (Bantam paperback, 1977), is fine for this activity.

(2) Clifford J. Wright and Graham Nuthall, "Relationships between Teacher Behaviors and Pupil Achievement in Three Experimental Elementary Science Lessons," *American Educational Research Journal,* Vol. 7, 1970, pp. 477-491.

(3) *Learning,* September 1975, p. 45.

(4) Idea suggested by a former "Personality of the Week," Christopher Hotz of Emerson, New Jersey.

(5) *"Instructor,"* December 1976.

(6) Dr. Girolama Garner (survey participant), "Modifying Pupil Self-Concept and Behavior," *Today's Education,* January 1974.

CHAPTER TWO

(1) Mrs. Wesner's curriculum is entitled "Life in a Nutshell," and is published by Education Electronics in Oklahoma City.

(2) Henry J. Hermanowicz, "The Pluralistic World of the Beginning Teacher," *Kentucky School Journal* 44, November 1965, and cited by Carol LeFever, "Teacher Characteristics and Careers," *Review of Educational Research* Vol, 37, No. 4, October 1967, p. 439.

(3) Mr. Oberparlieter can be contacted at 27 Hummingbird Lane, Willingboro, NJ, telephone 609-871-0917.

(4) *Learning,* April 1974. by Bruce Raskin, "Teacher Information Exchanges,"

(5) Gene I. Maeroff, "Coast Clearinghouse Helps Teachers Share Innovations," *New York Times,* February 11, 1977.

CHAPTER THREE

(1) Cook Caldwell, and Christiansen, *The Come-Alive Classroom,* Parker Publishing Co., Inc., 1967, pp. 1, 2.

(2) Idea further described by Mary M. Harris, survey participant, in *Instructor*, December 1974, p. 49.

(3) V.N. Campbell and M.A. Chapman, "Learner Control Versus Program Control of Instruction," *Psychology in the School*, 1967.

(4) Romaine Beidelman's idea is from *Instructor* magazine.

(5) From "Project Open Classroom," a program funded initially by the Elementary and Secondary Education Act, and described in *Educational Programs that Work*, Department of Education, Trenton, NJ, 1974-5, p. 68. Dr. Thelma Newman is program coordinator.

(6) "Four Days On; One Day Off!" *Scholastic Teacher*, September 1973.

(7) See also "Teacher Burnout," *Instructor*, January 1979, pp. 56-62.

CHAPTER FOUR

(1) Nicholas P. Crisuolo, "Centering in on Books and Life Sciences," *Teacher*, 1977.

(2) "A Very Real Science Class," *Instructor*, September 1975.

(3) *Learning*, February 1977.

(4) "Ticket to a Learning Center," *Instructor*, August-September 1975.

(5) Susan Scilla (staff writer), "High School Provides a Place for Graffiti" *The Record* (Hackensack, NJ), October 1975.

(6) Helen P. Silver, "Children Measure the Metric System," *New York Times*, October 19, 1975.

(7) John H. Kuhn (staff writer), "Students 'Fly' South," (Hackensack, NJ) *The Record*, March 19, 1975.

CHAPTER FIVE

(1) Ideas of Winnedfred M. Haugland, survey participant, further described in *Instructor*, April 1975.

(2) *NJEA Review*, published by the New Jersey Education Association, April 1975.

(3) *Pack-O-Fun* is a monthly scrap-craft magazine located at 14 Main Street, Park Ridge, IL 60068.

(4) *Instructor*, December 1975.

(5) Cook, Caldwell, and Christiansen, *The Come-Alive Classroom*, Parker Publishing Co., Inc., 1967, p. 14.

CHAPTER SIX

(1) "Compensatory Education Valuable at All Ages," *NJEA Review, April 1975*.

(2) Jon Shure (staff writer), "Schools Cheat Our Gifted Kids," *The Record*, January 12, 1977.

(3) Marcia Stamell (staff writer), "Cliff's Gifted to Be Allowed Study Freedom," *The Record*, June 11, 1975.

(4) "A Test to Leave School," *The Record*, December 1975.

(5) Tom Groenfeldt and Dave Stout (staff writers), "College Courses for High School Students," *The Record*, September 19, 1977.

(6) "Schools Cheat our Gifted Kids."

(7) Sandra Blakeslee, "Challenge for the Very Bright—A College for Kids," *New York Times*, May 21, 1975.

(8) "Last One Out," *Learning*, November 1976, p. 62; originally from *What's Going On Here*, a publication of the Springfield, Oregon, Public Schools.

CHAPTER SEVEN

(1) Dewey Lipe and Steven M. Jung, "Manipulating Incentives to Enhance School Learning," *Review of Educational Research*, Vol. 41, No. 4, p. 271.

(2) "Is IPI Built on False Assumptions?" *NJEA Review*, May 1975. "Copyright the New Jersy Education Association."

(3) Alison Wolf, "When the Teacher Should Keep Quiet," *Learning*, January 1977; study cited is M. B. Rowe, "Wait Time and Rewards as Instructional Variables: Their Influence on Language, Logic, and Fate Control," *Journal of Research in Science Teaching*, Vol. 11, No. 2, 1974.

(4) Brenda Pena (survey participant), "Pouches of Projects," *Instructor*, August-September, 1974.

(5) Edward E. Bowman (survey participant), "Solving Problems in English with AIDE" *N.J.S.D.C. Bulletin*, published by the New Jersey School Development Council, Vol. 20, Fall 1974, pp. 24, 25.

CHAPTER EIGHT

(1) Instructor, January 1977.

(2) Sister Mary Laubacher, "Cooperative Composition Correction," *Learning*, November 1976, p. 47.

(3) Scripts like these can be found in *Scholastic Scope* (Scholastic Magazines, 50 W. 44th St. New York, NY 10036). You might also want to read the *New York Times* article "TV Scripts Become Textbooks" (December 12, 1978, p. C5), and you can write to Cities Television Productions (4100 City Line Ave., Philadelphia PA 19131) for information on TV scripts.

(4) Article "Will the Mystery Guests Please Sign In," *Teacher*, January 1977.

(5) Cindy Kadonga, "He Makes Scientists Come Alive," *New York Times*, April 25, 1976.

CHAPTER NINE

(1) William Glasser, *Schools Without Failure*, Harper & Row, 1969, pp. 122-144.

(2) Jane Manzelli, "Motivation Is a Matter of Trust and Dialog," *Instructor*, January 1975.

CHAPTER TEN

(1) Gene I. Maeroff, "Pupils' Testing Lag Linked to Parents," *New York Times*, September 21, 1976.

(2) Michael P. Scott, "How Parents Are Learning to Help Kids Learn," *Better Homes and Gardens*, September 1977, pp. 10-14.

(3) Letha Kemp Smith, "Bridging Home and Kindergarten," *Instructor*, August-September 1975.

(4) Seth S. King, "Reading Plan Aids Poor Pupils in Chicago," *New York Times*, September 25, 1976.

(5) *Today's Education.*

(6) "Operation Gold Rush," *NJEA Review,* September 1976.

(7) Joseph A. Cobb, "Relationship of Discrete Classroom Behaviors to Fourth Grade Academic Achievement," *Journal of Educational Psychology,* Vol. 63, No. 1-74-80, 1972.

(8) Judith Cummings, "A Case of Slow Readers Leading the Slow Reader" *New York Times,* December 31, 1975.

(9) The Amity Aide program is based in DelMar, CA, 92014 (Box 118).

(10) *Reader's Digest,* December 1975, p. 52.

CHAPTER ELEVEN

(1) Jacob S. Kounin and Paul V. Gump, "The Comparative Influence of Punishment and Non-Punishment upon the Children's Concept of School Misconduct," *Journal of Educational Psychology,* 1961.

(2) Henry Clay Lingrne, *Educational Psychology in the Classroom,* fourth edition, John Wiley & Sons, Inc., 1972, p. 270.

(3) Jacob S. Kounin and Paul V. Gump, "The Comparative Influence of Punishment and Non-Punishment."

(4) "Judge Lets Guilty Set their Own Punishment—and Gets Few Repeat Offenders," *National Enquirer,* November 23, 1975.

(5) From a personal presentation by Dr. Glasser during a televised graduate course entitled "Human Relations and School Discipline," 1975.

(6) Mary M. Petrusich, "Give Them a Lesson for the Rest of Their Lives," *Instructor,* March 1975.

(7) L. W. Mc Allister, J. G. Stachowaik, D. M. Baer, and L. Condermon, "The Application of Operant Conditioning Techniques in a Secondary School Classroom," *Journal of Applied Behavior Analysis,* Vol. 2, 1969; cited by Lipe and Jung, "Manipulating Incentives to Enhance School Learning," *Review of Educational Research,* Vol. 41, No. 4, p. 259.

(8) Robert L. Spaulding, "Achievement, Creativity, and Self-Concept Correlates of Teacher-Pupil Transactions in Elementary Schools," A study supported by the U.S. Office of Education in 1963 and cited in *Learning,* February 1977.

(9) "How Do You Say It?", *Instructor,* April 1975.

(10) Jacob S. Kounin and Paul V. Gump, "The Comparative Influence of Punishment and Non-Punishment."

(11) Dr. William Glasser, "A New Look at Discipline," *Learning,* December 1974, pp. 6-11.

(12) William J. Cnagey, "Discipline, Classroom," *Encyclopedia of Education,* Vol 3, 1971; cited by Jean E. Davis, "Coping with Disruptive Behavior," published by the National Education Association, 1974, p. 21.

CHAPTER TWELVE

(1) *Encyclopedia of Education,* Vol. 4, 1971.

(2) Maya Pines, "You *Can* Help your Children Learn," *Reader's Digest,* January 1979, pp. 100-103.

(3) "Homework: What Research Says to the Teacher", an NEA (National Education Association) publication, 1975, pp. 23-4.

(4) "Homework: What Research Says to the Teacher", p. 24.

(5) George W. Bond, and George J. Smith, "Homework in the Elementary School," *National Elementary Principal*, January 1966.

(6) Kathryn Berry, "Homework," *Instructor*, February 1977.

(7) Encyclopedia of Education, Vol. 4, 1971.

(8) "Homework: What Research Says to the Teacher," pp. 19-20.

(9) John F. Check, "Homework—Is It Needed?", *The Clearing House*, Vol. 41 No. 3, 1966, pp. 143-147.

CHAPTER THIRTEEN

(1) Ruth Anne Olnowich, "A Study Concerning Attitudes of Students Toward Teacher-Made Tests," undergraduate research presented to the Department of Education at Glassboro State College, NJ, 1965.

(2) George G. Thompson, Eric F. Gardner, and Francis DiVesta, *Educational Psychology*, Appleton-Century-Crofts, 1959, pp. 95-6.

(3) See "Maculaitis Assessment: Proficiency Tests for Non-Native Students in Grades K-12 (MAC:K-12)" for other specific testing ideas.

(4) William Glasser, *Schools Without Failure,"* Harper & Row, 1969, p. 227.

(5) Gunnar Horn (survey participant), "Laughter . . . A Saving Grace," *Today's Education*, December 1972, pp. 27-28.

(6) James J. Berry and Wilbert M. Leonard III, "A Different Approach to Classroom Testing," *Today's Education*, November-December 1974.

(7) Ellis Batten Page, *Teacher Comments and Student Performance*, 1962; cited in Noll and Noll, eds., *Readings in Educational Psychology*, Macmillan, 1962, pp. 264-5.

CHAPTER FOURTEEN

(1) Cook, Caldwell, and Christiansen, *The Come-Alive Classroom*, Parker Publishing Co., Inc., 1967, p. 26.

(2) "Classroom Tips," *Today's Education*, September 1975.

CHAPTER FIFTEEN

(1) Gertrude Moskowitz and John L. Hayman, Jr., "Interaction Patterns of First-Year, Typical, and 'Best' Teachers in Inner-City Schools," *Journal of Education*, 1966.

(2) Philip V. Brennan, Jr., "Humor in the Classroom Pays Off—With Higher Grades," *National Enquirer*, November 23, 1976.

(3) Gunnar Horn (survey participant), "Laughter . . . A Saving Grace," *Today's Education*, December 1972, pp. 37-38.

(4) Dr. Norman Vincent Peale, known and loved for his *Power of Positive Thinking*, has written another best-seller entitled *Enthusiasm Makes the Difference,"* Fawcett Crest, 1967.

(5) Information on PEN can be obtained through June Betsworth, Hubbard Street Elementary School, Sylmar, CA.

(6) "On the Dearth of Good Teachers," letter to the editor, *New York Times*, December 8, 1975.

(7) "Mr. Harris Pays a Visit," *Teacher*, September 1976.

(8) Gunnar Horn (survey participant), "Education of a Teacher: Students Provide Liberal Curriculum," *Omaha World Herald,* May 7, 1972.

(9) Robert S. Soar, "Optimum Teacher-Pupil Interaction for Pupil Growth," *Educational Leadership,* 1968; cited by Alison Wolfe in "Myths of Education," *Learning,* February 1977.

(10) Robert R. Blake and Jane Srygley Mounton are authors of *Corporate Excellence Through Grid Organization Development,* Gulf, 1968, and other outstanding business books.

(11) This study is described fully in the *Journal of Teacher Education,* Fall 1975.

APPENDIX: STATISTICAL RESULTS OF TEACHER SURVEY

RESPONSES TO QUESTIONNAIRE ITEMS

Figures *above* boxes denote the percentages of those responding from the group of 311 A+ Teachers.

Figures *below* boxes designate the percentages of those responding from the group of 109 Other Teachers.

Asterisks (*) point out those differences between the two groups which are *statistically significant* according to the Chi-Square Test of Significance (.05 level of confidence).

A. WHAT GOALS DO YOU STRESS FOR YOUR STUDENTS?

	NEVER	SELDOM	SOMETIMES	OFTEN	ALWAYS
1. Learning, achieving academically (above)	0.0	1.3	10.0	36.9	51.8
1. (below)	0.0	1.0	4.9	29.4	64.7
2. Gaining practical skills (above)	0.0	0.3	6.9	35.4	57.4
2. (below)	0.0	1.9	4.7	32.7	60.7
3. Being neat, accurate, organized (above)	0.3	3.3	19.0	39.7	37.7
3. (below)	0.0	0.0	15.2	33.3	51.4
4. Questioning and seeking own answers* (above)	0.0	0.7	11.5	34.1	53.8
4. (below)	0.0	0.0	15.4	46.2	38.5
5. Developing talents and interests* (above)	0.0	1.0	9.5	41.1	48.4
5. (below)	0.0	1.9	23.1	32.7	42.3
6. Becoming involved in current issues* (above)	1.3	5.3	33.1	38.7	21.5
6. (below)	1.9	13.5	34.6	28.8	21.2
7. Developing a positive self-image* (above)	0.0	0.3	5.5	20.5	73.6
7. (below)	0.0	2.9	9.6	30.8	56.7
8. Being creative* (above)	0.3	1.0	18.4	34.8	45.6
8. (below)	0.0	7.8	22.3	37.9	32.0
9. Behaving in an acceptable manner (above)	0.0	1.3	7.9	25.0	65.8
9. (below)	0.0	0.0	3.8	18.9	77.4

B. WHERE DO YOU GET YOUR IDEAS AND INSPIRATIONS FOR SUBJECT MATTER, METHODS, ETC.?

	NEVER	SELDOM	SOMETIMES	OFTEN	ALWAYS
1. Commercial texts, programs, etc.	2.0 / 0.0	10.7 / 6.5	36.8 / 32.7	44.0 / 49.5	6.5 / 11.2
2. Curriculum guide*	6.5 / 17.5	22.9 / 17.5	39.5 / 29.1	26.1 / 29.1	4.9 / 6.8
3. Educational television	18.4 / 14.9	32.1 / 38.6	37.0 / 38.6	11.5 / 7.9	1.0 / 0.0
4. Workshops, courses, seminars*	0.3 / 4.8	9.7 / 19.2	33.4 / 37.5	48.4 / 34.6	8.1 / 3.8
5. Educational books, magazines, etc*	0.6 / 1.9	6.2 / 15.2	31.5 / 37.1	52.9 / 39.0	8.8 / 6.7
6. Holidays, events, special occasions	5.0 / 8.9	17.6 / 24.8	30.9 / 35.6	37.9 / 25.7	8.6 / 5.0
7. Your students*	1.3 / 1.0	3.6 / 15.2	37.2 / 48.6	47.6 / 29.5	10.4 / 5.7
8. Other teachers*	1.0 / 0.9	8.4 / 12.1	46.1 / 49.5	41.9 / 29.0	2.6 / 8.4
9. Your own creative ideas	0.0 / 0.0	0.7 / 0.0	16.0 / 17.8	59.0 / 62.6	24.4 / 19.6

C. WHAT MAGAZINES AND PERIODICALS DO YOU READ?

	NEVER	SELDOM	SOMETIMES	OFTEN	ALWAYS
1. American Teacher	56.3 / 65.5	14.6 / 16.7	16.0 / 13.1	7.3 / 3.6	5.8 / 1.2
2. Changing Education*	43.2 / 56.8	15.0 / 18.5	24.1 / 17.3	12.3 / 2.5	5.5 / 4.9
3. Instructor*	19.3 / 33.7	10.8 / 12.0	27.0 / 29.3	22.8 / 14.1	20.1 / 10.9
4. Learning*	38.0 / 49.4	11.5 / 18.5	17.9 / 16.0	12.4 / 8.6	20.1 / 7.4
5. Scholastic Teacher	25.4 / 37.1	17.1 / 21.3	26.3 / 24.7	22.1 / 11.2	9.2 / 5.6
6. Teacher (Grade Teacher)*	29.7 / 46.5	8.8 / 8.1	20.5 / 18.6	24.5 / 17.4	16.5 / 9.3
7. Today's Education (NEA)	5.8 / 5.8	3.1 / 3.8	19.9 / 26.9	30.5 / 28.8	40.8 / 34.6

Which book has influenced your teaching most?_____

D. HOW DO YOU PLAN AND PREPARE YOURSELF?

	NEVER	SELDOM	SOMETIMES	OFTEN	ALWAYS
1. Use commercial planbook*	36.0 / 20.2	12.5 / 9.6	10.0 / 14.4	8.7 / 16.3	32.9 / 39.4
2. Follow teacher manuals	13.8 / 8.8	22.8 / 21.6	26.5 / 30.4	28.9 / 32.4	8.1 / 6.9
3. Establish objectives for the year	2.0 / 2.9	4.3 / 5.8	11.5 / 19.2	30.6 / 25.0	51.6 / 47.1
4. Make long-range plans (month or more)*	4.7 / 3.9	9.3 / 17.5	17.3 / 26.2	32.3 / 25.2	36.3 / 27.2
5. Plan weekly	1.3 / 3.9	2.3 / 2.9	12.5 / 6.8	25.1 / 29.1	58.7 / 57.3
6. Plan daily	3.1 / 5.8	8.8 / 9.6	8.5 / 8.7	23.1 / 22.1	56.5 / 53.8
7. Use spur-of-the-moment teaching opportunities*	1.0 / 3.8	8.8 / 9.4	26.9 / 44.3	38.0 / 26.4	25.3 / 16.0
8. Plans checked by principal or supervisor	48.0 / 55.4	15.3 / 12.9	13.0 / 9.9	6.3 / 8.9	17.3 / 12.9
9. Plan with students*	3.2 / 8.6	8.1 / 20.0	39.9 / 50.5	40.9 / 14.3	7.8 / 6.7
10. Plan with other teachers	6.6 / 2.8	20.7 / 23.6	34.5 / 38.7	32.6 / 30.2	5.6 / 4.7

E. HOW IS YOUR CLASSROOM SET UP?

	NEVER	SELDOM	SOMETIMES	OFTEN	ALWAYS
1. Desks in rows*	36.3 / 45.0	10.0 / 5.0	18.9 / 12.5	21.9 / 12.5	13.0 / 25.0
2. Desks in groups	23.0 / 27.1	9.4 / 9.4	27.7 / 28.2	25.9 / 14.1	14.0 / 21.2
3. Tables instead of desks	34.3 / 35.2	7.5 / 3.4	14.6 / 12.5	7.8 / 11.4	35.8 / 37.5
4. Displays of student accomplishments*	3.1 / 8.8	5.8 / 11.0	15.9 / 15.4	24.4 / 25.3	50.8 / 39.6
5. Learning centers*	17.1 / 31.0	11.5 / 13.8	18.9 / 18.4	19.6 / 11.5	32.9 / 25.3
6. Exhibits*	5.1 / 13.8	11.6 / 18.4	24.9 / 23.0	29.4 / 23.0	29.0 / 21.8
7. Specialized work areas (Math, etc.)	18.3 / 33.3	10.1 / 7.1	21.9 / 15.5	19.1 / 16.7	30.6 / 27.4

	NEVER	SELDOM	SOMETIMES	OFTEN	ALWAYS
8. Live animal(s)*	43.2 / 62.5	15.7 / 7.5	15.7 / 8.8	11.1 / 6.3	14.3 / 15.0
9. Plants	22.7 / 30.2	9.8 / 4.7	16.4 / 16.3	18.2 / 15.1	32.9 / 33.7
10. Chalkboards that are utilized	1.0 / 0.0	1.7 / 1.1	9.3 / 5.4	18.5 / 22.6	69.5 / 71.0
11. Bulletin boards that are utilized	1.0 / 2.0	2.7 / 1.0	7.7 / 6.1	17.1 / 25.5	71.6 / 65.3

F. WHAT MATERIALS AND EQUIPMENT DO YOU USE?

	NEVER	SELDOM	SOMETIMES	OFTEN	ALWAYS
1. Camera	22.3 / 30.1	15.1 / 17.2	28.1 / 30.1	26.3 / 14.0	8.3 / 8.6
2. Tape recorder*	6.6 / 7.1	7.6 / 13.1	24.1 / 34.3	38.0 / 26.3	23.8 / 19.2
3. Phonograph*	6.9 / 6.9	4.9 / 12.7	17.8 / 39.2	39.8 / 25.5	30.6 / 15.7
4. Motion pictures	1.0 / 1.9	5.9 / 4.7	20.8 / 29.9	48.2 / 44.9	24.1 / 18.7
5. Opaque or overhead projectors	8.0 / 6.7	14.3 / 6.7	30.2 / 31.7	31.6 / 39.4	15.9 / 15.4
6. Ditto masters and machine	2.6 / 0.0	3.6 / 2.8	16.5 / 17.0	39.9 / 40.6	37.3 / 39.6
7. Commercially produced games, kits	11.2 / 14.9	16.5 / 18.8	27.1 / 36.6	32.7 / 20.8	12.5 / 8.9
8. Newspapers, catalogs, magazines	3.3 / 8.7	7.9 / 8.7	33.9 / 38.5	36.2 / 30.8	18.8 / 13.5
9. Scraps, left-overs, etc.*	8.5 / 12.8	13.3 / 28.7	26.6 / 24.5	31.4 / 23.4	20.1 / 10.6
10. Teacher-made materials	5.6 / 7.2	5.9 / 10.3	17.0 / 18.6	39.3 / 43.3	32.2 / 20.6
11. Student-made materials*	9.7 / 18.6	17.8 / 29.1	30.0 / 23.3	25.9 / 20.9	16.6 / 8.1

G. HOW DO YOU ALLOW FOR INDIVIDUAL DIFFERENCES IN YOUR STUDENTS?

	NEVER	SELDOM	SOMETIMES	OFTEN	ALWAYS
1. Vertical grouping (different ages, grades)	27.0 / 38.0	17.3 / 8.7	22.7 / 17.4	17.6 / 17.4	15.5 / 18.5
2. Using multi-level materials	6.1 / 5.8	3.1 / 9.6	21.7 / 22.1	35.3 / 33.7	33.9 / 28.8
3. Stressing individual growth and achievement*	0.3 / 1.0	0.3 / 2.9	5.9 / 17.1	26.0 / 29.5	67.4 / 49.5
4. Homogeneous groupings within class	8.9 / 12.0	10.6 / 12.0	32.9 / 20.0	28.4 / 33.0	19.2 / 23.0

5. Enrichment for gifted students*

1.7	2.7	15.0	40.0	40.7
3.9	6.8	25.2	35.0	29.1

6. Extra help for slow learners*

0.0	1.9	7.1	35.0	56.0
0.9	2.8	14.8	30.6	50.9

7. Activities for individual talents, interests*

0.7	2.9	16.0	36.3	44.1
1.0	6.7	34.6	29.8	27.9

H. WHAT TEACHING METHODS DO YOU USE?

	NEVER	SELDOM	SOMETIMES	OFTEN	ALWAYS

1. Formal class lessons

4.1	12.0	34.6	38.7	10.6
2.9	11.8	28.4	46.1	10.8

2. Class discussions*

0.7	1.6	19.6	54.6	23.5
0.0	6.7	27.6	50.5	15.2

3. Team-teaching

33.1	21.3	24.0	14.3	7.3
29.7	27.7	22.8	13.9	5.9

4. Small-group instruction*

2.3	6.5	29.4	42.2	19.6
5.7	15.2	25.7	34.3	19.0

5. Individualized approach*

2.3	6.2	24.7	38.6	28.2
7.4	13.0	26.9	25.9	26.9

6. Following texts and other sequential materials

5.3	9.9	34.8	39.1	10.9
3.8	11.4	34.3	35.2	15.2

7. Relating all work to over-all themes

2.7	8.0	24.3	43.0	22.0
4.9	10.8	27.5	38.2	18.6

8. Contracting with students

27.1	20.2	28.4	19.9	4.5
35.6	16.3	27.9	12.5	7.7

9. Commercially prepared programs

16.1	24.5	40.9	16.1	2.3
27.2	15.5	38.8	14.6	3.9

10. Drill work*

9.6	16.8	36.6	28.7	8.3
13.1	10.3	36.4	23.4	16.8

11. Memorization

8.0	28.1	45.8	15.7	2.3
13.3	21.9	46.7	13.3	4.8

12. Innovative or original methods

4.1	2.0	35.2	34.7	24.0
3.3	8.2	44.3	31.1	13.1

I. WHAT ACTIVITIES OR LEARNING EXPERIENCES DO YOU OFFER YOUR STUDENTS?

	NEVER	SELDOM	SOMETIMES	OFTEN	ALWAYS

1. Creative writing

12.2	9.7	24.0	31.9	22.2
17.6	15.4	26.4	29.7	11.0

2. Role-playing, drama*

13.5	11.1	30.1	29.4	15.9
29.2	13.5	24.0	24.0	9.4

3. Setting up bank, store, etc. in the classroom

30.1	20.9	26.7	13.4	8.9
38.9	14.4	21.1	20.0	5.6

4. Contests, games, competitions*

6.0	11.9	26.8	37.4	18.2
12.9	17.8	33.7	25.7	9.9

5. Small-group or committee work*

NEVER	SELDOM	SOMETIMES	OFTEN	ALWAYS
3.3	8.4	29.1	44.5	14.7
9.1	11.1	40.4	29.3	10.1

6. Field trips*

NEVER	SELDOM	SOMETIMES	OFTEN	ALWAYS
6.6	14.6	35.9	28.6	14.3
11.9	22.8	40.6	18.8	5.9

7. Guest speakers*

NEVER	SELDOM	SOMETIMES	OFTEN	ALWAYS
7.7	20.5	38.4	21.9	11.4
13.5	29.2	42.7	10.4	4.2

8. Practical, hands-on activities

NEVER	SELDOM	SOMETIMES	OFTEN	ALWAYS
7.1	6.2	24.6	32.2	29.9
10.1	10.1	25.8	28.1	25.8

J. HOW ARE YOUR STUDENTS ACTIVELY INVOLVED IN THEIR LEARNING?

1. Class meetings*

NEVER	SELDOM	SOMETIMES	OFTEN	ALWAYS
13.6	15.0	38.0	21.6	11.8
26.3	24.2	30.3	12.1	7.1

2. Participating in planning and directing*

NEVER	SELDOM	SOMETIMES	OFTEN	ALWAYS
5.7	13.0	47.2	25.8	8.4
12.5	36.5	35.6	9.6	5.8

3. Freedom of movement and expression*

NEVER	SELDOM	SOMETIMES	OFTEN	ALWAYS
0.0	3.3	22.4	43.4	30.9
1.9	7.5	38.7	34.9	17.0

4. Choosing individual endeavors*

NEVER	SELDOM	SOMETIMES	OFTEN	ALWAYS
2.3	5.4	31.1	46.8	14.4
6.7	11.5	43.3	26.0	12.5

5. Correcting papers*

NEVER	SELDOM	SOMETIMES	OFTEN	ALWAYS
14.8	19.5	34.7	25.6	5.4
28.3	20.2	31.3	16.2	4.0

6. Keeping independent records of progress*

NEVER	SELDOM	SOMETIMES	OFTEN	ALWAYS
8.7	14.7	36.7	26.0	14.0
18.6	19.6	27.5	20.6	13.7

7. Periodic conferences with you*

NEVER	SELDOM	SOMETIMES	OFTEN	ALWAYS
1.0	7.9	32.0	42.6	16.5
7.6	14.3	36.2	26.7	15.2

8. Striving for rewards and awards*

NEVER	SELDOM	SOMETIMES	OFTEN	ALWAYS
7.8	13.3	35.8	29.4	13.7
14.6	23.3	32.0	22.3	7.8

9. Using equipment and audio-visual aids

NEVER	SELDOM	SOMETIMES	OFTEN	ALWAYS
3.7	9.0	23.6	39.2	24.6
2.9	16.2	21.9	40.0	19.0

10. Classroom jobs and responsibilities

NEVER	SELDOM	SOMETIMES	OFTEN	ALWAYS
3.0	9.4	18.4	35.1	34.1
4.8	13.3	20.0	29.5	32.4

11. Creating bulletin boards, exhibits

NEVER	SELDOM	SOMETIMES	OFTEN	ALWAYS
5.3	10.3	30.0	31.3	23.0
6.9	16.7	30.4	23.5	22.5

12. Celebrating birthdays, special occasions*

NEVER	SELDOM	SOMETIMES	OFTEN	ALWAYS
14.4	12.4	26.2	24.8	22.1
34.0	18.0	18.0	11.0	19.0

K. WHO ELSE IS ACTIVELY INVOLVED IN TEACHING YOUR STUDENTS?

1. Other teachers and specialists

NEVER	SELDOM	SOMETIMES	OFTEN	ALWAYS
12.2	13.9	22.6	22.6	28.7
12.6	15.5	25.2	20.4	26.2

2. Principal*

NEVER	SELDOM	SOMETIMES	OFTEN	ALWAYS
44.3	25.1	20.6	5.9	4.2
70.3	13.9	10.9	3.0	2.0

3. Students (peer teaching)

NEVER	SELDOM	SOMETIMES	OFTEN	ALWAYS
9.6	13.7	36.9	31.7	8.2
14.4	19.2	39.4	19.2	7.7

4. Classroom aide*	46.0	13.9	15.7	13.9	10.5
	72.0	7.0	12.0	7.0	2.0
5. Student teacher, college helper*	32.5	12.3	30.1	18.8	6.2
	41.7	17.5	28.2	10.7	1.9
6. Parents*	40.5	21.1	24.6	10.7	3.1
	71.3	15.8	8.9	4.0	0.0
7. Volunteers*	44.6	20.4	19.6	13.7	1.8
	67.3	15.8	12.9	4.0	0.0

L. HOW DO YOU HANDLE DISCIPLINE PROBLEMS?

	NEVER	SELDOM	SOMETIMES	OFTEN	ALWAYS
1. Small reminders (look, snap of fingers, etc.)	3.4	6.7	25.2	45.6	19.1
	1.9	5.8	26.2	40.8	25.2
2. Verbal reprimand	3.6	10.9	48.7	29.8	7.0
	1.9	7.4	42.6	38.0	10.2
3. Punishment (written work, separation, detention, withholding privileges, etc.)*	26.7	28.7	29.7	13.5	1.4
	13.2	25.5	33.0	23.6	4.7
4. Involving principal, school disciplinarian*	31.0	47.0	18.7	3.0	0.3
	14.2	41.5	32.1	11.3	0.9
5. Involving parents*	12.9	34.4	34.1	16.2	2.3
	4.7	26.2	34.6	26.2	8.4
6. Ignoring bad behavior while encouraging good	11.0	15.7	38.8	27.1	7.4
	10.5	21.0	42.9	19.0	6.7
7. Private conference with offender(s)	1.0	3.2	25.3	48.4	22.1
	0.0	2.8	31.8	43.9	21.5
8. Involving class in solving problem*	16.4	21.4	38.5	20.4	3.3
	25.2	28.2	35.9	7.8	2.9
9. Have student(s) work out problem independently*	8.8	23.7	46.8	16.6	4.1
	17.5	32.0	43.7	3.9	2.9

M. HOW DOES HOMEWORK ENTER YOUR EDUCATIONAL PICTURE?

	NEVER	SELDOM	SOMETIMES	OFTEN	ALWAYS
1. Written assignments*	14.0	22.9	34.2	22.3	6.5
	7.9	10.9	28.7	33.7	18.8
2. Study or preparation assignments*	12.1	17.9	34.1	30.3	5.5
	5.0	9.9	35.6	36.6	12.9
3. Same assignment for all	16.4	18.4	30.7	28.0	6.5
	14.1	16.2	35.4	20.2	14.1
4. Individualized assignments	8.2	12.6	46.9	26.9	5.4
	12.9	8.9	45.5	21.8	10.9
5. Free-choice assignments*	14.8	16.9	44.8	20.3	3.1
	29.3	28.3	35.4	4.0	3.0
6. Assignments for those who want it*	22.0	17.5	38.5	17.8	4.2
	43.9	21.4	24.5	5.1	5.1

7. Assignments for those who need it

12.4	10.7	41.4	26.9	8.6
16.3	11.2	29.6	27.6	15.3

8. Text or workbook assignments*

22.3	17.5	30.2	24.1	5.8
12.7	9.8	34.3	35.3	7.8

9. Skill or drill assignments

13.2	16.6	41.4	23.4	5.4
11.0	13.0	42.0	27.0	7.0

10. Creative assignments*

5.1	10.4	40.1	36.0	8.4
10.0	14.0	50.0	24.0	2.0

11. Long-range assignments (a week or more)

20.5	14.4	27.7	28.1	9.2
18.2	21.2	34.3	21.2	5.1

N. HOW MUCH TIME PER WEEK DOES A STUDENT IN YOUR CLASS SPEND ON YOUR ASSIGNED HOMEWORK?

	None	Less than 1 hour	1-5 hours	5-10 hours	More than 10
Weekly estimate	9.4	33.4	51.9	5.2	0.0
	4.0	28.0	63.0	5.0	0.0

O. HOW DO YOU USE TESTS?

	NEVER	SELDOM	SOMETIMES	OFTEN	ALWAYS
1. To determine student progress	2.3 / 0.0	3.3 / 0.9	23.7 / 20.8	42.0 / 46.2	28.7 / 32.1
2. To motivate effort and achievement*	7.4 / 2.9	12.1 / 5.8	32.6 / 29.8	34.9 / 40.4	13.1 / 21.2
3. To encourage memorization of facts	18.6 / 14.7	33.8 / 27.5	32.8 / 35.3	13.1 / 17.6	1.7 / 4.9
4. To test understanding of concepts, processes	2.4 / 1.9	2.7 / 1.0	19.9 / 12.5	49.7 / 46.2	25.3 / 38.5
5. To see what student knows (e.g., pre-test)	2.0 / 0.9	9.7 / 8.5	33.6 / 34.9	39.6 / 29.2	15.1 / 26.4
6. To set up instructional groups*	9.2 / 15.7	18.8 / 16.7	34.2 / 30.4	29.8 / 20.6	7.9 / 16.7
7. To reinforce students' test-taking skills*	13.0 / 11.9	26.7 / 27.7	31.2 / 32.7	25.3 / 16.8	3.8 / 10.9
8. To evaluate your own teaching	2.3 / 1.0	5.0 / 5.7	25.2 / 23.8	35.4 / 37.1	32.1 / 32.4

P. HOW MANY TESTS DOES A STUDENT IN YOUR CLASS TAKE PER WEEK?

	0	1 or 2	3-5	5-10	More than 10
Weekly estimate	14.8	66.1	17.3	1.8	0.0
	12.8	64.9	19.1	1.1	2.1

Q. HOW DO YOU KEEP STUDENT PROGRESS RECORDS?

	NEVER	SELDOM	SOMETIMES	OFTEN	ALWAYS
1. Relying on memory	57.4 / 65.3	21.1 / 17.9	13.8 / 11.6	5.5 / 4.2	2.1 / 1.1
2. Commercial marking or grading book*	18.3 / 7.8	5.1 / 2.9	12.2 / 9.8	19.3 / 11.8	45.1 / 67.6
3. Teacher checklists of completed tasks, mastered skills, etc.*	7.0 / 11.8	7.0 / 14.7	21.4 / 11.8	38.5 / 34.3	26.1 / 27.5
4. Individual student folders or files*	12.8 / 17.5	3.9 / 10.7	18.8 / 17.5	27.0 / 16.5	37.5 / 37.9
5. Classroom displays of progress charts, etc.*	30.4 / 48.0	19.6 / 14.3	24.7 / 17.3	16.6 / 7.1	8.8 / 13.3
6. Anecdotal records	26.4 / 37.0	13.0 / 18.0	28.8 / 17.0	18.2 / 15.0	13.7 / 13.0
7. Own original system	35.1 / 37.3	10.3 / 13.4	19.5 / 19.4	17.3 / 14.9	17.8 / 14.9

R. WHICH CHARACTERISTICS DESCRIBE YOU IN THE CLASSROOM?

	NEVER	SELDOM	SOMETIMES	OFTEN	ALWAYS
1. Well-organized	0.7 / 0.0	2.3 / 0.9	13.8 / 18.5	46.2 / 41.7	37.0 / 38.9
2. Strict	2.3 / 1.9	8.1 / 10.4	39.9 / 34.9	34.2 / 32.1	15.4 / 20.8
3. Consistent	0.3 / 0.0	2.0 / 0.0	9.9 / 11.3	43.4 / 48.1	44.4 / 40.6
4. Soft-spoken	2.3 / 0.0	8.9 / 9.7	36.0 / 45.6	35.6 / 32.0	17.2 / 12.6
5. Creative	0.0 / 0.9	2.6 / 3.7	30.9 / 38.3	37.2 / 37.4	29.3 / 19.6
6. Enthusiastic*	0.0 / 0.0	0.0 / 0.0	4.6 / 10.3	37.3 / 44.9	58.2 / 44.9
7. Humorous*	0.0 / 0.0	1.3 / 10.3	26.1 / 30.8	46.3 / 36.4	26.4 / 22.4
8. Patient, understanding	0.3 / 0.0	1.6 / 0.9	11.8 / 13.0	49.2 / 54.6	37.0 / 31.5

S. HOW MUCH OF YOUR *OWN* TIME DO YOU SPEND ON SCHOOL-RELATED WORK EACH WEEK?

	None	Less than 5 hours	5-10 hours	10-20 hours	More than 20
Weekly estimate	0.7 / 0.9	5.6 / 6.6	35.4 / 49.1	41.1 / 32.1	17.2 / 11.3

T. HOW MUCH OF YOUR OWN MONEY DO YOU GENERALLY SPEND FOR SCHOOL MATERIALS PER SCHOOL YEAR?

	Less than $10	$10-$25	$25-$50	$50-$100	More than $100
Yearly estimate*	10.7	20.8	24.4	19.9	24.1
	32.1	20.8	30.2	9.4	7.5

U. IN WHICH ORGANIZATIONS DO YOU PARTICIPATE?

	NEVER	SELDOM	SOMETIMES	OFTEN	ALWAYS
1. Parent-Teacher Association*	23.7	6.1	12.5	12.5	45.2
	9.9	16.8	27.7	12.9	32.7
2. NEA, other educational associations*	7.3	3.0	12.6	16.2	60.9
	10.8	8.8	18.6	18.6	43.1
3. Educational committees*	3.6	5.6	18.0	34.4	38.4
	12.1	12.1	32.3	22.2	21.2
4. School voluntary activities*	2.3	3.4	21.1	38.9	34.2
	5.0	9.0	33.0	31.0	22.0
5. Tutoring programs	26.1	23.0	27.8	16.5	6.5
	24.5	23.5	29.6	16.3	6.1
6. Civic affairs*	6.7	12.1	30.3	28.3	22.6
	21.6	25.8	32.0	13.4	7.2
7. Service organizations*	11.6	16.0	29.0	22.5	20.8
	27.7	23.4	24.5	16.0	8.5
8. Little league, scouts, etc.	43.0	18.7	21.8	8.5	8.1
	59.4	12.5	13.5	7.3	7.3
9. Religious school staff*	39.7	11.5	17.8	11.1	19.9
	68.1	8.8	9.9	9.9	3.3

V. DO THE FOLLOWING FACTORS CONTRIBUTE TO YOUR TEACHING SUCCESS?

	NOT AT ALL	A LITTLE	SOMEWHAT	QUITE A BIT	VERY MUCH
1. College training*	1.0	9.4	28.3	31.3	30.0
	3.8	12.4	37.1	21.0	25.7
2. Student teaching experience	11.3	18.6	23.6	23.9	22.6
	8.8	13.7	22.5	26.5	28.4
3. Past experience as a teacher	0.6	0.3	1.9	19.7	77.3
	0.0	0.0	4.7	16.8	78.5
4. Rapport with class*	0.0	0.0	2.6	22.3	75.1
	0.0	0.0	5.6	35.2	59.3
5. The teaching methods you use	0.0	0.3	10.1	39.1	50.5
	0.0	0.9	11.0	43.1	45.0

6. Effort and hard work*

0.0	0.3	3.5	26.5	69.7
0.0	0.0	10.3	26.2	63.6

7. Working well with others (parents, staff, etc.)

0.0	0.6	9.4	30.1	59.9
0.0	1.9	13.1	33.6	51.4

8. The number of students in class

9.4	8.4	19.8	28.6	33.8
5.7	7.6	20.0	27.6	39.0

9. The type of students you teach

8.7	13.3	21.7	26.5	29.8
6.7	4.8	30.8	24.0	33.7

10. Your personal appearance

5.6	11.8	36.3	24.5	21.9
3.7	9.3	31.8	29.0	26.2

11. Enjoyment of job

0.0	0.0	1.9	13.6	84.4
0.0	0.9	0.9	20.6	77.6

INDEX

U

Unifield Mathematics and Metrics, 19
Unplanned activities, 29-30
Uses, 45-46

V

Vespe, Vincent J., 156
Volunteers in classroom, 123-124
  "Amity Aides," 127
  archeological expeditions, 124
  former students, 123
  interviewing excursions, 124
  local residents, 123
  retired teachers, 123
  school personnel, 127
  senior citizens, 123
  students at nearby colleges, 124
  teachers in educational television, 127
Von der Linden, Mildred, 134

W

Ward, Wanda, 106
Watson, Sharon A., 6, 18, 21, 29, 123, 147, 157, 177

Webster, Barbara, 99, 106, 116, 136, 179
Weekly plan sheet (sample), 28
Wesner, Maralene, 3, 8, 53, 147, 187
Wheel of concern, 74
Widerberg, Willard C., 70, 76, 138
Widicus, Edith, 98
Willey, Betty B., 144
Wilson, Donald R., 97
Winkler, Mrs. Ray, 3, 44, 54, 102
Wolf, Margaret, 52, 100
Wolfe, Rinna, 6, 9, 30, 34, 69-70, 71, 97, 119, 137, 184, 186, 188
Word party, 80
Word study card (exhibit), 72

Y

Yearbook, 188
"Yellow Pages" resource book, 8

Z

Zeichner, Charles, 45, 87, 101, 106, 137, 166
"Zephros," 20
Zuzov, Ann, 3, 113